Wiley Study Guide for 2019 Level III CFA Exam

Volume 4: Alternative Investments, Risk Management, & Derivatives

Thousands of candidates from more than 100 countries have relied on these Study Guides to pass the CFA® Exam. Covering every Learning Outcome Statement (LOS) on the exam, these review materials are an invaluable tool for anyone who wants a deep-dive review of all the concepts, formulas, and topics required to pass.

Wiley study materials are produced by expert CFA charterholders, CFA Institute members, and investment professionals from around the globe. For more information, contact us at info@efficientlearning.com.

Wiley Study Guide for 2019 Level III CFA Exam

Volume 4: Alternative Investments, Risk Management, & Derivatives

WILEY

ISBN 978-1-119-53088-6

V092629_100518

Contents

ABOUT THE AUTHORS

Wiley's Study Guides are written by a team of highly qualified CFA charterholders and leading CFA instructors from around the globe. Our team of CFA experts work collaboratively to produce the best study materials for CFA candidates available today.

Wiley's expert team of contributing authors and instructors is led by Content Director Basit Shajani, CFA. Basit founded online education start-up Élan Guides in 2009 to help address CFA candidates' need for better study materials. As lead writer, lecturer, and curriculum developer, Basit's unique ability to break down complex topics helped the company grow organically to be a leading global provider of CFA Exam prep materials. In January 2014, Élan Guides was acquired by John Wiley & Sons, Inc., where Basit continues his work as Director of CFA Content. Basit graduated magna cum laude from the Wharton School of Business at the University of Pennsylvania with majors in finance and legal studies. He went on to obtain his CFA charter in 2006, passing all three levels on the first attempt. Prior to Élan Guides, Basit ran his own private wealth management business. He is a past president of the Pakistani CFA Society.

There are many more expert CFA charterholders who contribute to the creation of Wiley materials. We are thankful for their invaluable expertise and diligent work. To learn more about Wiley's team of subject matter experts, please visit: www.efficientlearning.com/cfa/why-wiley/.

Study Session 15: Alternative Investments for Portfolio Management

READING 30: ALTERNATIVE INVESTMENTS FOR PORTFOLIO MANAGEMENT

Time to complete: 14 hours

Reading summary: Alternative investment is an important asset class. Most institutional and many individual investors have added major alternative asset classes (e.g., hedge funds, private equity, real estate, commodity investments, managed futures, and distressed securities) to portfolios. Portfolio managers should, therefore, understand alternative investments and their role in portfolios in order to effectively serve investors.

This lesson will provide you with the tools to:

- Compare various alternative investment classes, including their benefits and drawbacks, and group them by the role they play in an investor's portfolio;
- Explain the process of investing in alternative investments, investment manager compensation structures, and unique charges and costs common to such investments;
- Understand the due diligence "checkpoints" necessary to evaluate alternative investments;
- Establish alternative investment benchmarks and evaluate and interpret performance against such a benchmark.

LESSON 1: ALTERNATIVE INVESTMENTS: DEFINITIONS, SIMILARITIES, AND CONTRASTS

Candidates should master the following concepts:

- Understand the common features of alternative investments;
- Explain the major due diligence checkpoints in selecting active managers of alternative investments;
- Understand issues that alternative investments raise for investment advisors of private wealth clients;
- Distinguish principal classes of alternative investments;
- Understand issues with benchmark selection for alternative investments.

LOS 30a: Describe common features of alternative investments and their markets and how alternative investments may be grouped by the role they typically play in a portfolio. Vol 5, pp 7–13

LOS 30f: Evaluate the return enhancement and/or risk diversification effects of adding an alternative investment to a reference portfolio (for example, a portfolio invested solely in common equity and bonds). Vol 5, pp 7–13

Common Features

Alternative investments can be described as:

- Possessing a return premium to compensate investors for relative illiquidity;
- Offering diversification benefits via relatively low correlation with a portfolio of stocks and bonds; and
- Difficult to evaluate due to benchmark construction complexities.

LOS 30d: Distinguish among types of alternative investments. Vol 5, pp 7–13

Classifications

Private equity, commodities, and real estate were *traditional alternatives* to bond and stock investments. Hedge funds, managed futures, and distressed securities are *modern alternatives*. Distressed securities may be considered:

- Private equity if private debt is considered part of private equity;
- Event-driven strategies under hedge fund investing; or
- A separate strategy.

These classifications tell us little about how to use such investments, so it may be more useful to categorize strategies according to their role in the portfolio:

- Exposure to *risk premiums* for factors not available via stock and bond investments (e.g., real estate, long-only commodities);
- Exposure to alpha by highly talented portfolio managers (e.g., hedge funds, managed futures); and
- Combinations of the first two (e.g., private equity, distressed securities).

LOS 30b: Explain and justify the major due diligence checkpoints involved in selecting active managers of alternative investments. Vol 5, pp 10–11

Due Diligence

Alternative investments may result in greater costs as investors engage in due diligence required by complex strategies and investment structures, opaque reporting, or special investigative skills. Checkpoints for traditional active management also apply to alternative investments, but the latter may require additional expense:

- **Market opportunity**—This can be especially true for venture capital investments.
- **Investment process**—Selection processes of investment managers dealing in areas where public information may be incomplete, such as private equity.
- **People and organization**—Alternative investments often require professionals with highly specialized skills, and some investments center on unique qualities that may be irreplaceable (e.g., venture capital).
- **Terms and structure**—Interests must be aligned to protect investors and avoid agency problems.
- **Service providers**—Attorneys, accountants, consultants, etc. may be very focused on a particular strategy or product area and command a premium.
- **Documents**—This may require additional investigation due to complexities in deal structure or process.

LOS 30c: Explain distinctive issues that alternative investments raise for investment advisors of private wealth clients. Vol 5, pp 11–13

Managers engaged by private clients rather than institutions should also be concerned with:

- **Suitability**—In some cases, money is "locked up" in an alternative investment for several years and may not be suitable for individuals with a short-term need.
- **Client communication**—Discussing complex structures and processes associated with alternative investments may be more difficult with private clients who are used to more traditional investments.
- **Decision risk**—The risk of a client exiting an investment at the point of maximum loss increases when the investment is complex, spans different life cycle periods, may have periods of loss in the early years, etc. Advisors should be especially careful to help investors understand the risk as part of determining suitability, and communicate effectively with clients during the life of the investment.
- **Taxes**—Alternative investments often have distinct tax issues to consider.
- **Concentration**—Advisors should be particularly aware of how private equity investments correlate with the client's business interests, or how real estate investments correlate with principal and second homes. In other words, the investments should be considered as part of the private investor's *total* portfolio.

LESSON 2: REAL ESTATE

Candidates should master the following concepts:

- Understand strengths and weaknesses of direct equity investment in real estate.

REAL ESTATE

This lesson focuses on equity investments in real estate rather than also including debt securities and mortgage debt held by individuals.

The Real Estate Market

Real estate has always been part of institutional and private portfolios outside the United States. Within the U.S., real estate performance depends heavily on tax laws related to deductibility of interest and passive loss limitations. Deregulation of the savings and loan industry as well as development of structured products based on principal and interest payments from buyers dramatically increased capital available for real estate investment. Recent risk limitations (Solvency II, Basel III, etc.) have dramatically decreased capital available for real estate investment.

LOS 30g: Describe advantages and disadvantages of direct equity investments in real estate. Vol 5, pg 21

Investors may participate directly by owning property or indirectly (i.e., financial ownership) through investment in:

- Homebuilders.
- *Real estate operating companies* (REOCs)—Own and manage properties.

- *Real estate investment trusts* (REITs)—Publicly traded equity securities with equity or debt investments in real estate. REITs must have at least 75 percent of their assets in real estate investments and pay at least 90 percent of earnings as dividends to shareholders.
- *Commingled real-estate funds* (CREFs)—Professionally managed pools of real estate investment capital that may be organized as either open- or closed-end (i.e., closed after an initial period) funds. Closed-end funds often employ greater leverage and have higher return objectives.
- *Separately managed accounts*—An investment account offered by a brokerage firm in which owned assets are managed by the brokerage or an outside firm. These are often offered as an alternative to CREFs.
- *Infrastructure funds*—A public entity hires a private consortium to design, build, finance, and operate an infrastructure project such as roads, bridges, hospitals, etc. The consortium then leases the project to the public entity for the duration of the agreement to do so. These consortiums will usually securitize the investment by selling shares in order to recapture its capital for use on the next project.

LOS 30e: Discuss the construction and interpretation of benchmarks and the problem of benchmark bias in alternative investment groups.
Vol 5, pp 15–19

Benchmarks

Analysts can often use publicly available information to develop a benchmark against which they can measure performance of a real estate portfolio. Private equity real estate, however, will tend to lag publicly traded securities and thus will not track well against such benchmarks. This can lead to a conclusion that real estate investments are uncorrelated with other investments, but this could be a misperception based on how prices for the properties have been determined.

NAREIT (National Association of Real Estate Investment Trusts) publishes a real-time, market-cap weighted index of REITs actively traded on the New York Stock Exchange and the American Stock Exchange. NAREIT also publishes other indexes with various timing and constituent qualities, but the aforementioned is the most prominent indirect equity investment index. FTSE EPRA/NAREIT publishes a Global Real Estate Index of securitized investments. The NAREIT indexes are generally considered investable.

Where the NAREIT Index investments may include 50 percent or greater leverage, the NCREIF (National Council of Real Estate Industry Fiduciaries) Index represents quarterly reported values for underlying investments as if they were not leveraged. The great majority of properties in the NCREIF Index have been acquired for pension funds and other fiduciaries, and the index is comprised of private equity investments in commercial real estate. These are considered direct investments in real estate.

Where REITs have relatively high return and high standard deviation (owing in part to the leverage), private equity investments will tend to have lower returns with lower volatility (owing to smoothing effects of less frequent appraisals). Unsmoothing the NCREIF increases returns and volatility, but the correlation between the unsmoothed NCREIF and NAREIT indexes is 0.71. Other comparisons show an overall low correlation between unsmoothed direct investment (NCREIF) and unhedged indirect investment (NAREIT).

For the period 1990–2004, real estate equity investments outperformed the S&P 500 Index and GSCI (Goldman Sachs Commodities Index) on a risk-adjusted basis. However, the NCREIF index is not investible because it represents unique, privately held properties.

Characteristics and Roles

Characteristics

Owners receive benefits from owning real estate; therefore, it has intrinsic value. Real estate also has financial benefits such as cash flow during the holding period and a potential capital gain at the end of the holding period. This differentiates real estate from hedge funds, which are more of an investment strategy, and makes it more like a direct investment in physical commodities, which also have tangible value.

Physical properties are immobile and the market may be illiquid with infrequent transactions in a particular property. It will also be heterogeneous (i.e., all properties are unique), have relatively high transactions costs, and the seller will know more about the property than the buyer *(asymmetric information)*. This latter characteristic can mean high returns and lower risk to investors who obtain high-quality information at a reasonable cost. Real estate values are heavily dependent on location, with complete diversification possible only by investing internationally.

Returns to real estate are positively correlated with economic growth, and inversely related to interest rate levels. Demographic factors such as population size and age also determine more or less the volume, price, and type of real estate sales. Conclusions on real estate's value as an inflation hedge are mixed. U.S. REITs had some long-term but no short-term inflation hedging ability.

Direct equity investments in real estate have advantages and disadvantages that with some exceptions (i.e., tax-related issues) apply to both individual and institutional investors. Advantages include:

- Mortgage loans allow greater leverage than possible with other types of equity investment.
- Mortgage interest, property taxes, and expenses are deductible to taxable investors.
- Direct investment allows control over various aspects of the property.
- Real estate in different locations can have low correlation and may provide diversification benefits.
- Good risk-adjusted returns.

Disadvantages include:

- Real estate investing may create large idiosyncratic (i.e., non-systematic) risk for investors if it represents a great proportion of assets in a portfolio and should be diversified.
- Problems affecting a property owner's neighbors may decrease the owner's property value.
- Each property is unique, requires separate due diligence, and therefore attracts higher investigation costs.
- Real estate requires maintenance and property repairs.
- Real estate brokers charge high commissions relative to brokers dealing in other assets.
- Tax benefits are subject to being discontinued (i.e., political risk).

Roles

Portfolio managers may use economic data on changes in expected GDP growth, real interest rates, the term structure of interest rates, and unexpected inflation to dynamically allocate to real estate investments, which tend to follow economic cycles. Therefore, real estate investments can be actively managed.

Real estate has been *less* affected by short-term changes in economic conditions than stocks and bonds, lowering correlation with those asset classes. Tenant lease payments also enhance return and lower volatility and correlation with other investments. REITs were less effective than hedge funds and commodities in diversifying a stock/bond portfolio and did not further diversify a portfolio already diversified with hedge funds and commodities. Direct investments provided *limited* additional diversification benefits over hedge funds and commodities. Within the real estate asset class, portfolio managers should be aware that large office buildings, warehouses, and industrial buildings are more affected by economic fluctuations than are investments in residential real estate, which also tends to be inflation resistant. Correlations across geographic areas tend to be high, suggesting that investors should diversify between metro areas and non-metro areas rather than simply concentrating in metro areas across geographical areas.

Both direct and indirect investments in the U.S. and elsewhere have exhibited non-normal distribution of returns. The jury is still out on why persistence (positive returns following positive returns, negative returns following negative returns) rather than a random walk occurs in the direct market but not in the indirect market.

Example 2-1

Jeffrey Endicott is CIO for Dagmar James Trust (DJT), a London-based foundation, which would like to diversify its investments. DJT has successfully used tactical asset allocation for many years to help grow the portfolio at a faster rate. In order to avoid expected volatility over the next four quarters, Endicott has suggested adding private equity real estate investments to reduce portfolio risk over the next year and returning to a higher small cap allocation at the end of that time. Darren Edwards, one of the board members, has opposed the move. Edwards' best argument against Endicott's suggestion is that private equity investments:

A. may take time to liquidate.

B. will not provide the necessary diversification benefits.

C. provide returns in line with bonds and will therefore set back the foundation's funding commitments.

Solution:

A. The fund uses tactical asset allocation, which requires opportunistically changing the asset allocation. Private equity real estate investments, however, are illiquid. This will be problematic when the fund returns to a greater equity allocation at the end of the year because the foundation may not be able to quickly sell out of the real estate investment. Private equity real estate can provide returns greater than a balanced bond/stock portfolio while reducing the standard deviation of returns from the portfolio.

LESSON 3: PRIVATE EQUITY/VENTURE CAPITAL

Candidates should master the following concepts:

- Discuss issuers and suppliers of venture capital, and stages through which private companies evolves;
- Compare venture capital to buyout funds;
- Understand convertible preferred stocks in venture capital investments;
- Explain structure of a private equity fund and compensation scheme;
- Understand private equity investment strategies.

LOS 30h: Discuss the major issuers and suppliers of venture capital, the stages through which private companies pass (seed stage through exit), the characteristic sources of financing at each stage, and the purpose of such financing. Vol 5, pp 27–34

PRIVATE EQUITY/VENTURE CAPITAL

Private equity securities are directly placed with institutions or individuals without first publicly issuing shares. Most institutions automatically qualify to purchase private issues although individuals must be *accredited investors* meeting net worth and income requirements under a country's securities laws. *Private equity funds* sell shares to investors and purchase private equity placements. Private equity investments may require a commitment of several years, so the pooled interest shares of a private equity fund may be much more liquid than the underlying privately placed shares.

Two types of private equity investment examined here are *venture capital funds*, which invest in startup or very new companies, and *buyout funds*, which take established public companies private.

In other cases, a public entity wishing to access capital during a period where its share price is low may opt for private investment in public equity (PIPE). In a PIPE, the private equity fund purchases shares directly from a publicly-traded company rather than from an underwriter or syndicate, thus avoiding high issuance costs and additional exchange scrutiny. This may be facilitated via warrants that allow the private equity funds to convert warrants to shares at some point.

Private Equity Markets

Most investors participate in private equity through private equity funds (indirectly) rather than directly. Buyout funds in recent years have seen capital commitments about two to three times that of venture capital funds. Where formative stage companies may shop their business plan to various potential direct investors, they may also raise funds through an agent using a private placement memorandum.

In any case, the supply and demand perspectives within the market for different types of funding offer reasonable insight to the market.

LOS 30i: Compare venture capital funds and buyout funds. **Vol 5, pp 30–33**

Venture Capital

Demand for venture capital is often driven by reasons associated with various stages of venture development:

- *Formative stage*—Includes newly formed companies with no more than an idea *(seed stage)*, start-ups beginning to develop the product *(start-up stage)*, and companies just beginning to sell a developed product *(first stage)*.
- *Expansion stage*—Includes companies needing working capital to expand sales, middle market companies with significant revenue, and companies preparing to make their initial public offering (IPO). Funding for expansion stage companies is generally known as *later-stage* financing.
- *Exit stage*—Firms in this stage are preparing to cash out initial investors via IPO, be acquired, or merge with another company.

These stages are further segmented in Exhibit 3-1. At any stage of its development, the new venture may go out of business and the venture capital providers may lose part or all of their investment.

Exhibit 3-1: Venture Capital Funding Timeline

	Formative Stage			Expansion Stage		
	Early Stage			Later Stage		Pre-IPO
	Seed	Startup	First Stage	Second Stage	Third Stage	Mezzanine (Bridge)
Characteristics	Idea, first hires, and prototype	Operations begin First revenues		Revenue growth		IPO preparation
Providers	Founders, FF&F*, angels, venture capital	Angels, venture capital		Venture capital, strategic partners		
Purpose	Business formation and market research	Product development and initial marketing	Working capital for manufacturing and sales	Initial expansion of marketing and production for established product	Capital for major expansion	Debt and equity capital to launch the company to the public

*FF&F = founders' friends and family.

The following groups supply venture capital:

- *Angel investors*—Accredited individual investors primarily involved with seed and early stage companies. Such investments are often the riskiest, especially if the investment occurs before organization or product development. Consequently, such investments will tend to be relatively small.
- *Venture capitalists*—Pools of money managed by venture capitalists (VCs) who specialize in the risks and rewards of companies that have potential, but may lack financial, marketing, and management expertise. Therefore, VCs often work side-by-side with management and join the board of directors.

  A venture capital fund is a single pool of investable funds. These may be privately or publicly held. A venture capital trust is a closed-end, exchange-traded vehicle that raises funds for venture investments.
- *Large corporations*—Large companies that invest in startups to complement their own strategic vision, thus often known as strategic partnering or corporate venturing.

Buyout Funds

Mega-cap buyout funds take larger public companies private. *Middle market buyout funds* purchase private companies that are too small to effectively access capital through public markets. In some cases these middle market companies may be spin-offs of larger companies or startups that have received some venture capital financing.

Buyout fund managers add value by:

- Identifying and purchasing companies below intrinsic value;
- Inserting their own specialists into the target or providing direction to improve strategic direction, operations, or management; and
- Re-capitalizing by adding debt or re-leveraging using lower cost debt.

Buyout funds realize a capital gain via IPO of the improved company or selling it to another company. In some cases, buyout funds engage in dividend recapitalization in which the firm adds debt and issues a special dividend to the owners.

Public employee pension plans provide the greatest dollar amount of funding, followed by private corporate pension plans, endowments, foundations, and family offices.

LOS 30j: Discuss the use of convertible preferred stock in direct venture capital investment. Vol 5, pp 34–35

Fund Structure and Return Provisions

Venture capital investors typically receive convertible preferred rather than common shares, with the provision that the target pay some multiple of original investment to the preferred shares before anything can be returned to common. This limits the possibility the owner/founders will receive a distribution on their common shares before the venture capitalists get paid. An acquisition event will trigger convertibility into common shares.

LOS 30k: Explain the typical structure of a private equity fund, including the compensation to the fund's sponsor (general partner) and typical timelines. Vol 5, pp 34–35

Also, subsequent rounds of venture capital financing have higher seniority of preferred status. This makes later round financing more valuable than each previous round, and senior to the founders' common shares. As a practical matter, however, valuation differences are slight and usually ignored.

PE funds often are structured as LPs or LLCs, with an expected life of 7–10 years, possibly extending for up to another 5 years. PE fund managers are charged with realizing investments by the end of fund life. Both LP and LLC forms allow cash flows and gains to flow to the investors without taxation at the entity level. The GP (or managing director of the LLC) receives a management fee of 1.5–2.5% of *capital committed*, including both employed and unemployed amounts, plus a performance incentive fee in the form of *carried interest*. Carried interest is the bonus (often 20 percent) due the fund manager after a return of capital to the investors and often after some percentage return *on* investor capital (the *hurdle rate* or *preferred return*). The carried interest percentage applies only to the profit after the hurdle rate.

In many cases, investors may be protected by a *clawback provision* that takes back bonuses already paid if subsequent investments fail to achieve the hurdle rate. Otherwise, investors are paid their hurdle, fund managers are paid their carried interest, and then investors receive the remaining profits.

For venture capital funds, the general partner (GP) selects and manages investments and commits its own capital in addition to the investors' capital commitment, which the GP takes down as required to purchase and manage investments. The limited partners (LPs) are protected from losing more than their invested amount.

The managing director of the LLC form must work with shareholders of the LLC in the amount of capital committed and when it is drawn down. This is therefore the preferred form for raising funds from a small group of investors with an interest in active management.

A PE fund of funds is an investment vehicle with money invested in several different PE funds. As with other funds-of-funds, the PE fund has a 0.5–2.0 percent management fee in addition to whatever the underlying funds charge.

Benchmarks

Returns for a private equity investment can be determined as the IRR for cash flows received during the investment and the cash out value. However, private equity can be difficult to benchmark because the underlying assets are not constantly bid on by a market of buyers. Other than failure of the project altogether, prices can be determined only when a financing event occurs (i.e., the underlying businesses access additional financing, have a public offer of shares, or are acquired). Benchmarks must estimate values using net asset value or residual value (in addition to the cash returns received) in order to estimate periodic returns.

Although short-term return and correlation may be affected by stale valuation estimates, returns are comparable and correlation is low with the general market for equity securities.

Correlations increase when biannual (every two years) data was used, indicating that data estimation and collection may in fact be at issue. There is no standard for appraisal and the underlying value is difficult to observe.

Economic conditions and market opportunities associated with the fund's year of inception may also be favorable or unfavorable, creating a "vintage year effect." Thus, funds from one vintage year are often compared only with other funds from the same vintage year.

LOS 30l: Discuss issues that must be addressed in formulating a private equity investment strategy. Vol 5, pp 38–43

Characteristics and Roles

Private equity investments typically share the following characteristics:

- *Illiquidity*—Convertible preferred shares received in venture capital deals do not trade in an active market, and buyout fund investments may be tied up for several years before it can be sold.
- *Long-term commitments*—Time horizons may be uncertain or long, and capital may be accessible during the lockup period.
- *Greater risk*—New and young companies have a greater failure rate than established firms, and consequently increase the risk of complete loss. Returns on PE investments show higher dispersion generally than public large cap investments, and may be compared to that for microcap stocks.
- *Higher IRR hurdle*—The required return for PE investments is higher than for public investments, owing to the higher risk, including lack of liquidity and marketability.

Venture capital investments will also tend to have little information regarding the market for a new product or for existing products with a new marketing approach or delivery method. Successful ventures, however, can generate outsize profits.

Discounts for lack of marketability (including discounts for lack of liquidity) may be combined with minority discounts where applicable. For a majority interest, the lack of marketability discount may include the additional aspect of selling a large block of shares.

Example 3-1

Billings Company has made a 10 percent minority investment in Calloway Industries. The intrinsic value for Calloway has been estimated at $75 million. Billings' investment banker has determined that a 20 percent discount for lack of marketability and a 15 percent discount for lack of control are appropriate. The value of Billings' nonmarketable minority interest, if each were calculated separately rather than combined, will be *closest* to:

A. $4.875 million.

B. $5.100 million.

C. $6.280 million.

> **Solution:**
>
> B. The value of the nonmarketable minority interest is (in $ millions):
>
> | | | |
> |---|---|---|
> | Controlling, marketable value | 7.500 | (75 × 10%) |
> | Discount for lack of control | (1.125) | (7.5 × 15%) |
> | Minority interest value | 6.375 | |
> | Discount for lack of marketability | (1.275) | (6.375 × 20%) |
> | Nonmarketable minority value | 5.10 | |
>
> Alternatively, this is 7.5 × (1 − 0.15) × (1 − 0.20) = 5.10

Buyout funds, however, have differences from venture capital funds:

- *Leverage*—Buyout funds typically have established cash flows that are often expected to improve, so can manage the 25–40% leverage typical for such an investment. Venture capital investments, however, typically use no leverage due to no or uncertain cash flows to service the debt.
- *Timing of cash flows*—Buyout investments receive cash earlier in the investment horizon and have less cash flow variability than venture capital investments. Venture capital investments have been said to follow a J-curve in which cash flows are negative during the early years and turn positive after five years or more.
- *Uncertainty of valuation*—Buyout investments typically have stable cash flows with less variability than venture capital investments, thus making their valuation easier than for venture capital investments.

> **Example 3-2**
>
> A foundation wishes to diversify its market-based investments by adding private equity. It has a 5–10 year time horizon for realizing its return, but wishes to have returns in excess of public equity securities and diversification from the public markets. Overall, it would prefer not to incur a loss of the entire investment. Which of the following types of private equity investment would best fit the foundation's risk-and-return parameters?
>
> A. Buyout fund.
>
> B. Seed investment in a company with a new social media concept.
>
> C. Venture capital trust investing in 8–10 highly promising companies.
>
> **Solution:**
>
> C. Although the buyout fund would likely provide a better return than public equity, the venture capital trust stands to provide the best return with risk diversified among 8–10 investments. The prospect of losing all capital in the venture trust is extremely low and one big winner will more than compensate for losses in a few others.

Portfolio Considerations

Although all companies have exposure to political, economic, and industry conditions (systematic risk), greater emphasis may be required on non-systematic risk when evaluating private equity investments. Even venture capital investments are subject to market conditions when the investors take the company public, but private equity overall provides diversification opportunities and high potential returns. Owing to the greater idiosyncratic risk, however, allocation to private equity in a well-diversified portfolio generally centers around 5 percent.

Private equity investment may be in the form of secondary purchases from current investors seeking liquidity as well as from investment in new PE funds. Issues to be addressed in formulating a private equity strategy include:

- *Ability to properly diversify*—Minimum private equity investments are usually $5 million. A private equity allocation should consider 5 to 10 investments requiring a $25 million to $50 million commitment. The total AUM should, therefore, be $500 million ($25mm/5%) or greater. Individual investors should consider investing in a fund of funds to properly diversify, although a second layer of fees will reduce the overall potential return.
- *Liquidity*—Private equity often has no liquidity for 7–10 years. Although a buyer for the locked up investment may appear, they will likely require a great discount to assume the position.
- *Capital commitments*—Capital calls may occur over 5 years or more.

Each fund may have a different diversification strategy depending on investments already in the portfolio. Private equity investments may be diversified by:

- Geography (e.g., country, region, etc.);
- Industry sector (e.g., technology, pharma, etc.); or
- Stage (e.g., seed, early, expansion, buyout, etc.).

Due Diligence

Due diligence concerns typically fall into these areas:

- *Strategic*—Evaluating the company's potential to compete in the market space;
    - *Prospects*—The ability of any company to make money in the space (e.g., growth, competition, supplier power, etc.).
    - *Products*—The ability of this company's product to satisfy customers, including analysis of customer opinions about the products. Leading neurosurgeons investing in a company making a new neurosurgery aid, for example, may be an indication of potential success.
    - *People*—Having the right people in place to implement the strategy, and properly aligning their goals with those of the company through compensation, bonuses, and ownership. A large financial investment by management of a target may indicate a deeper level of commitment to the company's ultimate success.

- *Financial/legal*—Examining all public and private financial documents, pending legal proceedings, intellectual property claims, etc.;
  - *Audit*—Investors may wish to audit financial statements themselves, especially in the case of seed and early stage companies which may not have audited financial statements.
  - *Performance review*—Fund performance should ideally be reported in compliance with Global Investment Performance Standards®. The investor should consider track record, consistency, fund manager capability, and team longevity.
- *Operational*—Investigating the company's internal processes for meeting strategy.
  - *Validation*—Investors should determine that the company's technology and processes will perform as expected.
  - *Intellectual property*—Investors should determine that the company owns the right to technology and processes, or has at least applied for patents and trademarks.
  - *Employment contracts*—Severance contracts, if exercised, should not be great enough to burden financial activities. Contracts should also keep key players in place long enough to ensure success.
  - *Dilution of interest*—Option grants should not be sufficient to compromise the investor's interests if the options are exercised.

LESSON 4: COMMODITY INVESTMENTS

Candidates should master the following concepts:

- Compare and contrast indirect and direct commodity investments;
- Understand the three components of a commodity futures contract;
- Understand the role of commodities in a portfolio.

LOS 30m: Compare indirect and direct commodity investment.
Vol 5, pp 46–47

Commodities

Commodities are relatively homogeneous tangible assets (e.g., gold, natural gas, oil, wheat, etc.) that by their nature lend themselves to standardized purchase and delivery contracts. A commodities-related investment is an alternative investment only when made via cash or derivative (futures) purchase of the commodity itself.

Direct commodity investments involve purchasing the commodity or futures and options on an underlying commodity. *Indirect commodity investments* involve purchasing a company that produces a commodity. Direct investments tend to expose investors to commodity price changes while indirect investments do not, presumably because the companies that produce the commodity have hedged most of their price risk off to speculators.

If an investor purchases the publicly traded security of a company in the commodities industry, it is an equity investment rather than an alternative investment in commodities. If an investor purchases a stake in a privately held company in the commodities industry, it is a private equity investment.

Markets

Commodity producers have been the primary players in commodities markets, with either cash positions (owning the commodity) or through participation in commodities futures (agreeing to future delivery). Commodity users often take the other side of the futures position, or purchase a cash position in the spot market. Investors may participate as *speculators*, taking the risk of price changes from producers, or as *arbitrageurs*, purchasing and selling commodities to opportunistically exploit market inefficiencies.

The futures market allows producers (sellers) to transfer price risk for future delivery to consumers or buyers of the commodity. In this way, futures markets increase efficiency in the spot market by allowing producers to make more of the product, some for delivery now and some for future delivery when it is needed. This may necessitate storage, which will be discussed shortly.

Futures positions may be closed out by the short party's delivery to the long position at maturity, or by *cash settlement* with a payment for the difference in the spot and contractual price. Most futures contracts are offset prior to maturity, which may be accomplished by selling the existing position (i.e., a long party sells her existing long position or a short party buys back his existing short position in the futures markets).

Benchmarks

Commodities are not traded worldwide in one centralized market, but information on worldwide prices may be obtained via investible commodity indexes. Investors may participate in funds based on commodity indexes such as Reuters Jeffries/Commodities Research Bureau (RJ/CRB) Index and S&P Goldman Sachs Commodities Index (S&P GSCI).

Returns from these indexes provide a benchmark for returns from passive long investments in the underlying futures, which are representative of spot prices based on the cost-of-carry model. The cost-of-carry model for fully-margined futures allows the index to mirror prices for spot delivery of commodities; that is, the commodity cost adjusted for the present value of storage costs should equal the futures price today, or arbitrage will ensue to bring spot and futures prices into line.

These indexes typically include energy, metals, grains, and soft commodities (e.g., cocoa, coffee, sugar, and cotton) but beyond that differ in composition, weighting scheme, and use. S&P GSCI, for example, is calculated primarily on a world production-weighted basis and comprises the principal physical commodities that are the subject of active, liquid futures markets. Monthly rebalancing of the GSCI is required to maintain replication, and differences in index returns can be explained by their components and weighting.

Overall, the indexes tend to underperform world bond and equity markets based on their Sharpe ratios, but have near-zero correlation with those asset classes. Commodities should not be considered a single homogeneous investment because commodity sector cross-correlations are also low. In addition, commodities included with another real asset class (such as a general "alternative investment") should be measured against an index appropriately weighted with all asset classes included in the designation.

Return Components

Investments in a physical commodity have no income component, so the return on a spot commodity investment will be a capital gain or loss. Futures returns have several components to consider:

Collateral Return

Collateral return assumes the investor posts a 100 percent margin on the futures contract in the form of T-Bills, thereby generating the risk-free rate.

Roll Return

A market is in *contango* when futures prices are higher than the current cash price (reflecting storage/insurance and interest costs). A market is in *backwardation* when futures prices are lower than the cash price (reflecting the premium paid by the seller to transfer price risk to the futures buyer).

Roll return (or *roll yield*) occurs when an investor sells a futures position just prior to maturity and "rolls" the proceeds into the next nearby futures contract. Roll return can be calculated as:

$$r_{Roll} = \frac{F_{t-1} - F_t - (S_t - S_{t-1})}{F_{t-1}} = \frac{\Delta F - \Delta S}{F_{t-1}}$$

Because futures prices equal the spot price plus the storage costs, then this should be some component of the futures price. However, next future contracts may have a different view of the attractiveness of holding the commodity. In essence, roll yield isolates the yield from rolling the futures forward from the change in futures price attributable to the change in spot price.

Example 4-1

A speculator is determining his returns from a September rough rice futures contract. The price of the futures contract was $14.42 in July and $14.50 in August. During that same period, the spot price declined by $0.08. The speculator will calculate a roll return (in USD) for July–August *closest* to:

A. −0.16

B. 0.00

C. 0.16

Solution:

C. Roll return is the change in futures price less the change in spot price:

$$r_{Roll} = F_{t-1} - F_t - (S_{t-1} - S_t)$$
$$= 14.50 - 14.42 - (-0.08) = 0.16$$

In *inverted markets*, an investor can earn a positive return using a simple buy-and-hold strategy as the lower futures price converges to the higher spot price. *Contango* markets, by contrast, can result in a negative roll return as the futures price falls toward the expected spot price.

This brings up the question of futures being an unbiased estimator of future spot prices, in which case there would be no roll return unless supply shocks or changes in demand occur.

Example 4-2

The April cash price for rough rice is $15.30. Rough rice futures contracts and each contract's open interest are:

May 20X1	$15.20	1713
July 20X1	$15.32	4717
September 20X1	$14.20	1390
November 20X1	$14.46	457

If futures prices are unbiased estimates of spot prices, buying May futures and holding them for the roll will *most likely* result in a:

A. loss.

B. gain.

C. push.

> **Solution:**
>
> A. Buyers have bid up the July futures contract price such that it is in contango while other contracts are inverted to the spot price. The July futures contract costs more than the May futures contract. Long futures generates a loss of $0.12. The spot price is expected to decrease from $15.30 to $15.20. Short spot is expected to generate a gain of $0.10. The total loss is expected to be $0.02 per contract. In this example, a seasonal commodity switching from backwardation (in which a roll return would be likely) to contango causes a slight loss.

Characteristics and Roles

Growth in world demand for what are largely limited resources tends to increase the value of a commodities investment over time. In addition, if equity security prices are in decline during periods of world economic turmoil (e.g., war in oil-producing countries), commodity prices may increase to reflect expectations of relative scarcity. Commodity price increases may also be behind price increases of finished goods that ultimately appear as inflation. Therefore, commodities provide not only diversification, but inflation protection.

LOS 30n: Describe the principal roles suggested for commodities in a portfolio and explain why some commodity classes may provide a better hedge against inflation than others. Vol 5, pp 51–55

Special Risk Characteristics

While commodity demand generally follows the business cycle, commodity prices are dependent on perceived short-term supply relative to demand. Stock and bond prices, however, are heavily dependent on longer-term expectations about the economy, inflation, and interest rates. Because of relative scarcity, commodities increase in value with inflation while stock and bond prices decrease as inflation rates increase, everything else being equal.

However, when stock and bond prices already reflect inflation expectations, commodity prices may increase together with stock and bond prices. Thus, the conclusion has been that commodity investments provide the greatest inflation hedge during periods of *unexpected* inflation.

Convenience Yield

Convenience yield reflects the embedded consumption-timing option in some commodities during certain periods, and can be expressed mathematically by adjusting the futures price formula:

$$F_{t,T} = S_t e^{(r+U-Y)(T-t)}$$

Convenience yields increase with a lower relative supply available. Although the volatility of cash prices may increase in the short term based on a mismatch between quantities supplied and demanded, in the long run supply and demand are somewhat flexible for commodities. Therefore, convenience yield has less importance as maturity increases.

Real Options

Producers hold options to produce or not produce a commodity, and will not exercise the option to produce if commodity prices are low. When spot prices are above discounted expected spot prices (i.e., futures prices in an inverted market), producers produce now in order to receive a higher price than if they wait.

Alternative Strategies

In addition to a hedge against unanticipated inflation, commodities (especially metals and agricultural products) may offer attractive returns during central bank tightening. A long-short strategy might be appropriate when a commodity's price is lower or higher than its underlying production cost. As price drops to cost plus margin, a short strategy will benefit. As price increases to cost plus margin, a long strategy will benefit.

LESSON 5: HEDGE FUNDS

Candidates should master the following concepts:

- Identify style classification of a hedge fund;
- Discuss fee structure of a hedge fund;
- Understand fund-of-funds;
- Discuss concerns in hedge fund performance evaluation.

HEDGE FUNDS

Although not statutorily defined, *hedge funds* can be thought of as pooled investment vehicles that attempt to implement a strategy, often taking advantage of a perceived inefficiency rather than benefiting from economic growth or competitive advantage as with traditional equity investments. Originally, hedge funds took long and short positions to remove market fluctuations at the expense of lower returns. Today, hedge funds are classified among many different strategies. Hedge funds often provide less protection to investors than other pooled investment vehicles and are not available to the general public.

Markets

Institutions and high-net-worth individuals (i.e., accredited investors) are the typical customers for hedge funds, although hedge funds in the U.S. are now being allowed to advertise to the general public. Firms offering prime brokerage services (i.e., leveraged trade execution, financing, accounting and reporting, securities lending, and start-up advice) actively compete for hedge fund business.

Although recent financial disruptions have collapsed many hedge funds, some have been able to return capital and new ones form each year. Many hedge funds claim their strategies defy benchmarking with absolute returns (i.e., returns on a particular asset without reference to other similar assets). Institutions often require a benchmark be created in order to measure fund performance.

LOS 30o: Identify and explain the style classification of a hedge fund, given a description of its investment strategy. Vol 5, pp 57–58

Classifications

Types of hedge fund investments include:

- *Market neutral*—Fund managers combine offsetting long and short positions within the same industry and market to extract return from company performance while "neutralizing" systematic risk. Not all investors are able to take short positions, however, and overvaluation will be slower to correct than undervaluation, meaning that timing for the gains from short positions and long positions in the same industry may differ.
- *Hedged equity*—Similar to market neutral in terms of buying good and shorting bad prospects, but often engaging concentrated positions without regard to offsetting positions or market neutrality. This strategy has the greatest assets under management (AUM).
- *Convertible arbitrage*—Exploit mispricing for convertible bonds, convertible preferred stock, and warrants. A simple strategy buys the undervalued convertible bonds and sells the overvalued stock associated with the convertible bonds. This separates the equity risk from the bond risk. The hedge fund earns additional return when the bond coupon exceeds the broker's margin interest rate. Because convertibles imply an option, bond prices may increase if the underlying stock volatility increases.
- *Fixed-income arbitrage*—Fund managers exploit mispricing based on their view of term structure, credit quality, or other bond-related variables. The long-short positions tend to neutralize systematic risk in the market.
- *Distressed securities*—Stocks and bonds of a financially distressed firm are often traded at a deep discount because risk-averse investors are willing to pay a hefty price to transfer risks of a distressed firm to others. Investing in a portfolio of deeply discounted distressed securities may yield abnormal returns.
- *Merger (deal) arbitrage*—This typically involves buying a target company's stock and shorting the acquirer's stock.
- *Global macro*—Assume systematic risk to capture movements in financial and non-financial assets (e.g., commodities, real estate, etc.) by investing in currencies, futures, options contracts, etc. in addition to long or short investments in stocks and bonds. Managed futures investments may be classified under global macro strategies owing to the category's use of futures.
- *Emerging markets*—These funds tend to be long because markets in less mature or developing countries often disallow short selling.
- *Fund of funds* (FOF)—An FOF will typically invest in 10–30 underlying hedge funds, which results in greater diversification but also requires paying management fees to the FOF sponsor as well as to the underlying funds.

Hedge funds have been classified by one index provider into:

- *Equity hedge*—Long and short equity positions regardless of net long-short exposure;
- *Debt hedge*—Long and short debt positions regardless of net long-short exposure;

- *Relative value*—Use long and short positions to exploit fair value divergence (e.g., equity market neutral, convertible arbitrage);
- *Event driven*—Opportunities created by corporate transactions (e.g., merger arbitrage) or financial distress;
- *Global asset allocation*—Long or short various financial and non-financial assets (e.g., currency, global macro including managed futures); and
- *Short selling*—Anticipates market decline.

LOS 30p: Discuss the typical structure of a hedge fund, including the fee structure, and explain the rationale for high-water mark provisions. Vol 5, pp 58–59

Fee Structure

Hedge funds generally receive a percentage of assets under management (i.e., an AUM fee) of 1–2 percent. Additionally, managers receive on average 20 percent of profits defined by the term sheet for the investment. In most cases, the profits must be based on a high-water mark (HWM), the greatest net asset value (NAV) achieved at a reporting date. This prevents managers from receiving incentive pay on the same return, such as during a downturn and subsequent recovery. In a "1-and-20" structure, for example, the manager receives a 1 percent AUM fee and 20 percent of the difference between reporting date NAV and HWM NAV. The reporting date NAV, if greater than the HWM, sets a new HWM. In a few funds, the incentive fee will be paid only in those periods where the change in NAV exceeds some hurdle rate.

Hedge funds far under the HWM may be dissolved because the manager will have little chance of earning an incentive fee. In some cases, funds allow investors to withdraw funds during downturns even though they may be in the *lockup period* that prevents withdrawal for, usually, 1–3 years.

Several arguments support the merit of high fund fee structures. One explanation delineates hedge funds receiving performance-based incentives on returns which often do not include market fluctuations. Another explanation is that the hedge fund supplies a protective put for which the manager should be compensated. Managers with better track records often receive higher fees.

Benchmarks and Performance

Several organizations offer active manager-based indexes, which they can use to benchmark performance. Tracking portfolios may also be available, which attempt to separate the manager's performance from strategy return. Although a manager may outperform the benchmark, the benchmark will be unlikely to provide a complete tracking portfolio for the hedge fund in part because hedge funds do not disclose their strategic and tactical allocations as transparently for fear of losing an edge in the market.

Many hedge funds claim *absolute return* characteristics, which cannot be used as a benchmark. However, estimates of *alpha* (return attributable to the manager's skill), which excludes returns to systematic risk, must be made with reference to a benchmark. Benchmarks that have traditionally been applied to long-only strategies may not be suitable because they fail to capture all sources of return from the strategy. Studies tend to show that active hedge-fund strategies deliver alpha, but there is usually no outstanding performance within any given strategy.

CSDIM's Hedge Fund Composite Index (HFCI) shows a higher Sharpe ratio relative to the S&P 500, corporate bonds, and world/global equities during the period 1990–2004. HFCI had a smaller decline than U.S. or world equities. During the market crisis from 2000–2002, HFCI showed a small positive trend.

Correlations of HFCI are highest with S&P 500 and world equities, but still below the correlation threshold to be considered worthwhile as a diversification tool.

However, different styles have markedly different risk-and-return characteristics. Styles neutralizing market risk tend to have low correlation with their respective stock or bond index counterparts. Event-driven and hedged equity styles tend to be more highly correlated with the S&P 500 index. Actual performance for a strategy will be in part driven by market conditions surrounding the strategy. For example, credit-sensitive strategies such as distressed securities will tend to reflect changes in high-yield debt securities. Equity hedge funds would be considered return enhancers rather than diversifiers because they bear so many return factor similarities.

Investors should consider the following factors regarding hedge fund indexes:

- *Creation bias*—Indexes should generally be created which indicate return from a generic version of the strategy. However, fund managers decide which indexes they will report to, which can lead to indexes that more closely follow the fund than the strategy and indexes based on the same style may have low correlations with one another. This could be due to size and age restrictions for the funds reporting or different weighting schemes.
  - ○ Value-weighted indexes may reflect popularity of a winning style;
  - ○ Equal-weighted indexes may be difficult and expensive to invest due to rebalancing costs;
- *Historical relevance*—Hedge funds change opportunistically, so comparing today's index with a prior period may be problematic, and this especially applies to value-weighted indexes (because they give greater weight to previous high performers). Additionally, studies show volatility is more persistent than the level of returns, meaning that forecasts consistent with prior volatility will be more reliable than forecasts consistent with prior returns.
- *Survivorship bias*—Indexes do not reflect the ongoing returns from funds that have failed. Therefore, indexes with high survivorship bias will tend to have higher returns than would be indicated by the average of all fund managers. This bias could be as high as 1.5–3.0 percent per year. FOFs may be able to avoid some survivorship problems by carefully performing due diligence on fund managers brought into the FOF.
- *Stale price bias*—Securities that trade infrequently (e.g., distressed securities) may have prices that fail to reflect the actual value of the securities. Studies suggest that this is not a serious problem in the hedge fund universe.

- *Inclusion (backfill) bias*—Also known as "instant history" bias, this results when a hedge fund joins an index and the index sponsor backfills the new constituent's history into the database. The fund manager has usually enjoyed a couple of successful years and has asked to join a database, the results of which are later added to the index. Thus, inclusion bias raises the bar for fund managers. This is not a serious bias, however, in many eyes because it is part of the data collection process.

Example 5-1

Alex Jones is examining several options for adding a market neutral long-short fund to the portfolio he manages for a foundation. He is concerned that the foundation's CIO will wish to see a benchmark against which they can measure the hedge fund's performance. Which of the following would Jones *most likely* recommend to replace the benchmark?

    A.   A hurdle rate.

    B.   A high-water mark.

    C.   A shorter lockup period.

Solution:

    A.   Market neutral long-short funds are absolute return funds that are difficult to measure objectively using a benchmark. However, a hurdle rate can help objectify the returns received by the foundation.

Characteristics and Roles

Skill-based investment strategies such as those employed by hedge funds gain their competitive advantage by superior information access or superior interpretation of publicly available information. However, the opportunity to gain and use information depends on the factors surrounding the strategy such as economic environment, legal and regulatory trends, and financial market conditions, etc.

Results of several empirical studies show that strategies favoring long positions tend to be driven by risk-and-return factors of the reference market. These strategies should, in a portfolio of long investments, be regarded as return enhancers rather than portfolio diversifiers. Strategies less affected by the general underlying factors of the reference market (e.g., market neutral long-short or arbitrage) make better portfolio diversifiers.

Roles in the Portfolio

A portfolio of 5–7 hedge funds has return and standard deviation characteristics similar to the universe of hedge funds with that strategy. Investing in an FOF reduces the manager selection process significantly. Studies have shown that even random selection of 5–7 hedge funds can result in correlation of 0.90 with a representative benchmark. In the end, a portfolio need not include the universe.

Example 5-2

Which strategy would *most likely* perform poorly in an illiquid market?

    A.   Distressed debt.

    B.   Merger arbitrage.

    C.   Market neutral long-short.

Solution:

    C.   Market neutral long-short funds require frequent rebalancing and adjustments based on changes in the relative value of firms within each industry. A lack of liquidity will increase trading costs and add expense to implementing the strategy. Distressed debt will often be more of a buy-and-hold strategy while workout is in process, and merger arbitrage requires selling the acquirer short (which provides liquidity) and buying the target (which requires liquidity), but the strategy is buy-and-hold so does not require frequent trading.

As stated elsewhere, mean-variance optimization (MVO) allocations are greatly influenced by the accuracy of return forecasts. Using historical returns in the MVO process may prove unreliable as well. Finally, some hedge fund strategies perform much like options, which do not fit nicely into MVO processes. While adding hedge funds to a traditional portfolio improves MVO outcomes, it may result in a greater number of negative outliers (negative skewness) and a greater number of observations in the tails (positive kurtosis or *leptokurtosis*), which are not attractive to investors.

Investors may be able to improve skewness and kurtosis outcomes in a portfolio by selecting funds that meet their needs. For example, global macro strategies tend to have high volatility, positive skewness, and high kurtosis, but have only moderate correlation with traditional equities. Equity market neutral strategies tend to have low kurtosis and low volatility. Managed futures tend to produce more favorable skewness and kurtosis outcomes and may be combined with other hedge funds to offset some of that risk.

Other Considerations

Investors in a hedge fund should consider several other factors:

- *Performance fees*—Severe downturns may cause collapse of the funds because fund managers are unlikely to meet high-water marks.
- *Fund size*—Large funds have advantages over smaller funds in attracting and retaining talented people as well as receiving more attention from the prime broker. However, smaller funds tend to outperform larger funds according to academic research, depending somewhat on the strategy employed. Smaller funds may, however, be more nimble and better able to take advantage of opportunistic purchases where a larger fund might move the market to its own disadvantage.

- *Vintage effects (fund age)*—Funds may not have the same opportunities at different times, so the median fund from the same vintage as a fund under investigation will provide a better reference point.
- *Liquidity*—Typically, investors must pre-notify a hedge fund of their intention to withdraw capital, with proceeds remitted to the investor at a later date specified by the fund.

LOS 30q: Describe the purpose and characteristics of fund-of-funds hedge funds. Vol 5, pg 58

A fund of funds will itself have several issues to consider:

- Survivorship bias should be less of an issue because discontinued funds will still affect the results for the FOF.
- Style drift may be more of a factor for FOFs because the manager is attempting to outperform, which may lead to higher correlation with standard indices as well as with general economic factors. As proof, hedge funds have become more aligned with hedged equity and less with global macro over time in an attempt to generate higher returns.

Due Diligence

Performing proper due diligence can help reduce portfolio risk. While hedge funds produce periodic performance reports, the proprietary nature of their strategies precludes them from disclosing positions. This means that reported performance cannot be tracked back to positions. Also, investors cannot check for risk exposure of hedge fund positions.

Example 5-3

Alpha fund is an opportunistic absolute value fund that a board member has recommended for inclusion in the hedge fund allocation along with 4 other funds. The *most likely* drawback of an allocation to a fund such as Alpha is:

    A.   strategy overlap.

    B.   manager tenure.

    C.   return persistence.

Solution:

    A.   Strategy overlap could become an important consideration as the opportunistic fund changes strategy toward the strategy with greatest return potential. The strategy change may duplicate what another fund in the portfolio already does, leading to an imbalance in the allocation. The other choices are possible issues but not likely given the information available.

LOS 30r: Discuss concerns involved in hedge fund performance evaluation. Vol 5, pp 60–70

Performance Evaluation Concerns

This section extends material on performance evaluation found elsewhere in the curriculum for issues specific to hedge funds.

Returns

Hedge funds report return as a nominal monthly holding period return:

$$r = \frac{NAV_t - NAV_{t-1}}{NAV_{t-1}} = \frac{NAV_t}{NAV_{t-1}} - 1$$

These monthly returns can then be compounded over 12 months to determine the annualized return. No compounding occurs on funds lost to the amount of an investor's drawdown, which may be quarterly or less frequently. Returns on assets controlled by derivatives provide a pseudo-return because they only require a minimal deposit to control the underlying. The convention in the hedge fund industry is to calculate return as if the underlying assets were fully owned.

Rolling return is the simple average of returns over the measurement period, usually current 12 months or annually:

$$RR_{n,t} = \left[r_t + r_{t-1} + \ldots + r_{t-(n-1)} \right] / n$$

Volatility

Standard deviation of monthly returns provides a measure of risk for hedge funds, much as with other types of investment. Annualized standard deviation, assuming a normal distribution and serially uncorrelated returns, equals the standard deviation of the monthly returns times the square root of 12. Hedge funds may violate the assumption of normal returns, especially with respect to the high number of low and high outliers.

Downside deviation (semideviation) uses only returns below an established threshold to calculate volatility. *Semideviation* uses average monthly return as the threshold, but zero or any other number may be used:

$$\text{Downside deviation} = \sqrt{\frac{\sum_{t=1}^{n} \left[\min(r_t - r^*, 0) \right]^2}{n-1}}$$

Min(A,B) means "smaller of either A and B."

Drawdown is another popular risk measure that considers the spread between the fund's high-water mark (HWM) and low asset value. The time it takes for a hedge fund to recover from a drawdown is relevant to determining hedge fund performance.

Performance Appraisal

The *Sharpe ratio* measures the excess return over a risk-free rate, usually the appropriate periodic U.S. Treasury bill yield, per unit of risk:

$$\text{Sharpe ratio}_j = \frac{(r_j - r_F)}{\sigma_j}$$

The Sharpe ratio has several limitations when used to measure hedge fund performance:

- *Lack of predictability*—A high Sharpe ratio cannot predict future success.
- *Time dependence*—Assuming no serial correlation of returns, an annual Sharpe ratio will be $\sqrt{12}$ times the monthly Sharpe ratio.
- *Stale pricing/illiquidity*—May result in trending returns, which lower variance of returns when the underlying asset value has not been reappraised.
- *Asymmetry*—Inappropriate for strategies with asymmetric distribution.
- *Correlation*—Fails to consider correlation of assets within a portfolio.
- *Gaming*:
    - Longer measurement intervals lower the standard deviation.
    - Compounding monthly returns, but using non-compounded monthly returns to calculate the Sharpe ratio.
    - Collecting premiums by writing out-of-the-money puts and calls that may not pay off for several years. Adding default risk, liquidity risk, or other types of risk that do not show up in the Sharpe ratio until they affect returns. This is similar to improving the mean or standard deviation by accepting greater skewness.
    - *Smoothing returns*—Illiquid or infrequently valued holdings result in an upward bias.
    - *Smoothing the tails* (smoothing volatility)—Using a total return swap or options to eliminate the high and low portfolio returns during the year to reduce volatility.

The *Sortino ratio* is similar to the Sharpe ratio, but measures the spread between return and minimum acceptable return (target return or *T*) divided by downside deviation *(DD)* over the period:

$$\text{Sortino ratio} = \frac{r_j - T}{DD}$$

The *gain-to-loss ratio* measures the relation of monthly gains to losses:

$$G/L \text{ ratio} = \frac{\#\text{monthly gains}}{\#\text{monthly losses}} \times \frac{\text{Average gain}}{\text{Average loss}}$$

Analysts should also consider *consistency* of results such that the fund has more positive returns relative to the index results. The time frame of rolling returns used to determine consistency should reflect the investor's holding period.

LESSON 6: MANAGED FUTURES

Candidates should master the following concepts:

- Understand trading strategies of managed futures;

Managed Futures Programs

Managed futures programs (MF programs or simply *managed futures)* are actively-managed pooled investment vehicles that may hold cash, spot, or derivative positions and may use leverage in a wide variety of strategies. Where global macro or other hedge funds tend to invest more heavily in spot markets and hedge these positions with derivatives, managed futures funds invest almost exclusively in futures, forward, or options markets. Where hedge funds focus on inefficiencies with respect to a single company's securities (micro basis), managed futures funds invest in derivatives representing a market basket of securities (macro basis).

LOS 30s: Describe trading strategies of managed futures programs and the role of managed futures in a portfolio. Vol 5, pp 84–88

Markets

MF programs are similar to many hedge funds in that they are absolute return vehicles that derive returns from the commodity pool operator (CPO's) trading skill. Limited partnerships of institutional or high-net-worth private investors (i.e., accredited investors) invest in a "pool" run by a general partner known as a commodity pool operator (CPO) and informed by commodity trading advisors (CTAs). However, MF programs are available for non-accredited investors. MF pools typically pay a 2 and 20 fee (2 percent AUM fee and 20 percent incentive fee) to the CPO.

The managed futures market in the U.S. has AUM approximately one-tenth the size of the hedge fund market, excluding managed futures pools held as part of a hedge fund or in institutional proprietary trading accounts.

MF programs are typically classified according to:

- *Style*: These strategies may be momentum or contrarian and further segmented by market:
    - *Systematic*—Rules-based trading strategies often based on historical pricing or trends.
    - *Discretionary*—Based on trader beliefs and economic conditions.
- *Market*:
    - *Currency*—Currency futures, options, and forwards.
    - *Financial*—Financial futures, options, and forwards.
    - *Diversified*—Currency, financial, and commodity futures, options, and forwards.
- *Strategy*:
    - *Momentum*—Choosing investments that have already been doing well (i.e., investing with market sentiment).
    - *Contrarian*—Choosing investments that may not have been doing well (i.e., investing against market sentiment).

Benchmarks and Performance

MF pool benchmarks generally attempt to replicate a CPO's or group's style or strategy. Benchmarks for actively managed strategies replicate the return to momentum- or contrarian-based mechanical trading rules for financial or commodities markets.

CTA$ Index, which follows various actively managed strategies, tends to have standard deviation of returns higher than bonds and lower than stocks, with Sharpe ratios better than stocks and worse than bonds. CTA$ Index has negative correlation with equity returns and moderate correlation with bond returns. Trend-following (momentum) MF investments tend to have the lowest correlation with discretionary style, as would be expected. Therefore, correlations for other style-market-strategy pairs tend to depend on whether they follow a momentum or contrarian strategy.

MF benchmarks may be subject to the same interpretation issues as hedge funds. Differences in return performance for surviving and non-surviving CTAs is greatest just prior to dissolution. Therefore, managers may achieve a distinct advantage by exiting investments in failing CTAs.

Characteristics and Roles

Because derivatives have a winner on one side and a loser on the other side of a trade, an unlevered passive pool will tend to return the risk-free rate less trading costs and management fees. Managed futures positions should be able to earn positive excess returns if hedgers on the other side of the trade are "paying a premium" to offset their risk. CTAs may also arbitrage market inefficiencies to achieve a return. These inefficiencies may occur as the result of different carrying costs or institutional differences.

Momentum strategies dominate actively managed pools, and may create positive skewness of return distributions. While equity market research has shown such strategies can generate excess returns, the results are mixed for such strategies in MF pools. Trading techniques that capture price trends from government policy intervention, or from corporate risk management policies, may produce excess returns.

Gains have been made in down as well as in up markets, and derivatives also allow positions that exploit volatility changes. Managed futures may provide investors access to returns not available through equity/bond or even equity/bond/hedge fund portfolios, and diversification opportunities that necessarily result.

MF performance depends on the investment vehicle, the time period, and the strategy. While publicly-traded commodities funds have shown poor portfolio *and* standalone results, CTA-managed pools tend to show valuable standalone *and* portfolio results. A random selection of 8–10 CTAs can provide the same results as a CTA-based managed futures index, which suggests an index can be used to develop asset allocation strategies even when the investor uses only a few CTAs.

The limited evidence showing performance persistence among CTAs is not strong enough to suggest that a strategy of investing in winners will provide excess returns over time. However, CTA beta provides a relatively good indicator of risk-adjusted performance over time.

Due diligence will be similar to that of hedge funds, with focus on risk management.

Example 6-1

Adding a managed futures portfolio to an efficient portfolio of bonds, stocks, and hedge funds will *most likely* cause the Sharpe ratio to:

A. increase.

B. decrease, because the portfolio is efficient.

C. decrease, because managed futures are similar to hedge funds.

Solution:

A. Adding an MF portfolio to an efficient portfolio of bonds, stocks, and hedge funds will most likely increase the Sharpe ratio. The low correlation with other asset classes will be likely to further reduce overall portfolio volatility, the denominator of the ratio, while potentially giving some improvement to the return measure. Hedge funds may be considered part of the hedge fund universe by some, but MF portfolios generally have quite low correlation with hedge funds generally.

LESSON 7: DISTRESSED SECURITIES

Candidates should master the following concepts:

- Discuss risks associated with distressed securities;
- Understand event risk, liquidity risk, market risk, and J-factor risk.

LOS 30t: Describe strategies and risks associated with investing in distressed securities. **Vol 5, pp 94–102**

Distressed Securities

Distressed securities are securities of companies in financial distress or bankruptcy and, as such, generally sell at a deep discount to the ongoing firm value. They range from securities that have recently fallen from investment grade to speculative status (i.e., fallen angels), to companies on the edge of bankruptcy, to actual bankruptcy proceedings, and even liquidation.

In the U.S., failed companies liquidate assets to pay debt under Chapter 7 and reorganize debt (to avoid liquidation) under Chapter 11 of the U.S. Bankruptcy Code. Investing in distressed securities involves considerable risk, especially in equity, which may lose all value in a restructure or liquidation. Returns to informed investors can be substantial, however, if the market has failed to accurately assess the situation. Investors may also be able to influence the reorganization or liquidation to favor their investments.

Markets

Because of these unique risk-and-reward characteristics, distressed securities do not behave like traditional debt or equity and are considered alternative investments. The major investors are typically private equity firms and hedge funds, primarily because of their flexibility to take both short and long positions in companies with speculative (rather than investment grade) status.

Structures

Although open end funds and separate accounts may be used to indirectly access distressed debt, the primary structures are:

- *Private equity funds*—Private equity funds provide a good structure for dealing with the illiquidity inherent in distressed securities because private equity investments often have long lockup periods. However, this limits investor liquidity. Private equity funds are also closed end (i.e., no new capital enters the fund after the subscription period). While this limits dilution to the investor's potential capital gain, closed-end funds suffer from the disadvantage of having little capacity to access additional capital after the initial subscriptions. Private equity managers often find it difficult to accurately forecast capital needs for distressed companies.
- *Hedge funds*—Hedge funds have the advantage of accessing additional capital, and investors have the advantage of greater flexibility in withdrawing capital. This may have led to hedge funds being the most popular structure for distressed security investment. However, illiquid or infrequently traded assets such as distressed securities make it difficult to reliably calculate fund NAV, which is used as the basis for AUM-based fees. Redemption rights may be inappropriate to offer in cases where this could limit the fund's ability to make additional investments as required by the nature of the distress.
- *Hybrids (private equity hedge funds)*—Allows illiquid and more liquid investments under the same fund structure, thus creating some withdrawal capability.

Asset Types
- The distressed company's public debt and equity.
- Bank debt and trade claims.
- *Orphan equity*—Equity issued to recapitalize a company emerging from bankruptcy. One study shows a 20 percent return versus relevant equity indexes over the first 200 days after emerging from bankruptcy.
- *"Lender of last resort" notes*—Central bank notes issued to stabilize a distressed firm when failure would jeopardize the financial system.
- *Derivatives*—Used to offset risk from a position.

Benchmarks and Performance

All major hedge fund indexes have a subcategory measuring distressed investment returns, often under the "event-driven' category. Distressed investments have high negative skewness, indicating a bias toward losses, and high kurtosis, indicating a higher than normal distribution of positive and negative results. However, the average return is quite positive and high. Based on this lack of normality, the Sharpe ratio may fail to reflect the risk/return tradeoff in a meaningful way.

For the period 1990–2004, distressed security investing outperformed the S&P 500 in terms of both return and risk. Distressed securities outperformed high-yield bond investments and performed better than all stock and bond investments over the period. Also, the minimum one-month return was less negative for distressed securities than for U.S. and world equities.

When the economy is not doing well, this strategy becomes more relevant and returns increase. However, the success of a distressed securities strategy hinges on the ability to predict events involved in the bankruptcy process, which likely leads to the high downside risk inherent in the strategy.

Analysts should be cautious to consider that the distressed securities market is perhaps the riskiest and most event-driven segment of high-yield bond indexes.

Characteristics and Roles

Portfolio optimization hinges on a variety of statistical techniques that rely on a normal return distribution. Distressed securities, owing to their high event risk, do not have a normal distribution. Relying on results as if returns were normally distributed will likely result in a lower return and higher standard deviation than expected. Therefore, investors will be more likely to choose distressed securities for return enhancement rather than for diversification purposes.

Distressed companies may be on the edge of slipping from going concern status, and thus investing in their securities may require specialized analytical skills, valuation experience, and the use of specialists (e.g., for legal evaluations). Valuation focuses not only on the going concern basis, but also on the liquidation value should the firm fail to emerge from reorganization.

Due diligence should consider not only the quality of underlying investments, but also the level of skill and resources possessed by a distressed securities portfolio manager.

Institutions hold an average of 5 percent of their portfolios in distressed security investments. Various strategies include:

- *Long-only investing*—High-yield debt or orphan equities investing are common.
- *Distressed arbitrage*—Holding the high-yield debt and shorting the equity. While the value of both debt and equity will decline if the company's prospects worsen, the strategy seeks to profit from the spread between the short equity and long debt positions. If the company's prospects improve, the strategy seeks to profit from the greater improvements in credit quality from the long debt position.
- *Active private equity*—The private equity investors purchase debt securities to obtain a position on the board or, if in bankruptcy, on the creditors' committee. The investors then actively seek improvements in the company's operations with the aim of improving the value of their investments. If investors receive shares as part of the bankruptcy process, the reorganization should enhance the share value.
- *Prepackaged bankruptcy*—The terms of the reorganization have been agreed before the formal process commences. This helps to lock in the profits expected by investors and helps reduce event risk from unfavorable legal outcomes, although there may still be creditors who may oppose the position accorded them in the prepackaged bankruptcy. In one variation, debt investors may acquire the equity of the failing company, which they rehabilitate and later IPO or sell to a private equity firm.

Practitioners of the active private equity approaches may be known as "vultures" and their funds are called "vulture funds" (in contrast to "venture" funds). In their defense, the vultures are assuming the risk of failure and potentially benefit society by rehabilitating failed companies.

LOS 30u: Explain event risk, market liquidity risk, market risk, and "J-factor risk" in relation to investing in distressed securities. Vol 5, pp 99–100

Specific risks include:

- *Market liquidity risk*—The risk an investor will be unable to withdraw money from the investment. This is an especially important risk, and somewhat influenced by the supply and demand cyclicality for such investments. These are non-systematic risks that contribute to low correlations with other asset classes.
- *Event risk*—Unexpected company- or situation-specific risks arising from the nature of the distress.
- *Market risk*—General systematic risks spanning economic activity, interest rates, equity market health, etc. This is less important than liquidity associated with the distressed equity markets specifically.
- *"J-factor" risk*—The judge's decisions will heavily influence the investment's success or failure. For example, judges can refuse to confirm a reorganization in which some creditors may receive less than under liquidation. Judges may disapprove on social or other grounds to a reorganization agreed by the creditors, forcing them to accept some other solution (i.e., the *cram down*).
- *Tax risks*—Various tax laws affect specific outcomes from the bankruptcy process. These are often secondary risks from event- and J-factor outcomes.
- *Asymmetric information risk*—The risk that others have more information about a particular process or outcome. The market for such investments closely scrutinizes the moves of vulture investors, and small changes in position or strategy may have a serious impact on other investors. Also, because many investors cannot invest in speculative investments, sell-side analysts seldom report on such situations, leaving a vacuum for experienced investors with this specialty.
- *Trustee decision*—A trustee in a bankruptcy proceeding administers the case, and could make unexpected or detrimental determinations.

Because these investments are often illiquid and difficult to value, stale pricing causes the risk of understating price volatility. Additionally, downward pressure by short-term vulture investors created by an unfavorable event can often make the deeply-discounted shares almost unsellable.

Example 7-1

Which of the following types of buy-side investor would most likely make an investment in distressed securities?

    A.   Pension fund.

    B.   Insurance company.

    C.   University endowment.

Solution:

    C.   In addition to attractive return possibilities, a university endowment has a long time horizon that would not be adversely affected by a long-term lockup such as required for distressed securities investing. The endowment will also be more likely to adjust its IPS to accept long-short investing that might be required for certain strategies within the distressed investments category. Insurance companies, however, may be restricted by state law from making speculative investments in the portfolio backing claims, and a pension fund will be subject to ERISA restrictions that likely prevent it from engaging in speculative investments altogether.

STUDY SESSION 16: RISK MANAGEMENT

READING 31: RISK MANAGEMENT

Time to complete: 14 hours

Reading summary: This reading focuses on the process of risk management. Risk management is an on-going process. We identify, measure, and manage risk factors in the business of investment management. We discuss features of the risk management process, outline the risk and return tradeoff, calculate value at risk (VAR), and interpret risk-adjusted performance measures, such as the Sharpe ratio and Sortino ratio. Candidates needs to understand and identify financial risk and non-financial risk, and be able to measure risks using volatility, beta, duration, delta, among other metrics. VAR is a key concept and candidates should be familiar with various methods to apply the concept. Risk-adjusted performance measures are important. Candidates should know how to interpret and compute these measures.

LESSON 1: RISK MANAGEMENT AS A PROCESS AND RISK GOVERNANCE

Candidates should master the following concepts:

- Understand risk governance, including the centralized and decentralized systems;
- Evaluate strengths and weaknesses of a company's risk management process;
- Describe steps in an effective enterprise risk management system;

RISK MANAGEMENT PROCESS

LOS 31a: Discuss features of the risk management process, risk governance, risk reduction, and an enterprise risk management system. Vol 5, pp 134–140

Traditional finance has focused on a key topic: how return is related to risk. The 1990 Nobel Prize winning model, the Capital Asset Pricing Model (CAPM), clearly states that expected returns on a security are directly related to the amount of systematic risk the security carries. However, in the business of investment management, there are many more risk factors than just systematic risk. Portfolio managers need to fully identify, measure, and control all possible risk factors. Risk managers need to understand risks that are worth taking and risks that should be avoided. Additionally, portfolio managers need to calculate, interpret, and report risk-adjusted returns to investors and other stakeholders, so that returns are not viewed in isolation. Risk-adjusted return measures are appropriate for reporting and comparison.

The collection of above activities is called the process of risk management. Note that risk management is not an action, but is a continuum of actions. The risk management process should be monitored, revised, and adjusted when they are needed. Successful risk management is a crucial part of investment management.

LOS 31c: Describe steps in an effective enterprise risk management system. Vol 5, pp 140–142

The process of risk management includes the following steps:

1. Identify risks. Risks include financial risks and non-financial risks.
2. Define risk tolerance. Level of risk tolerance depends on clients and management.
3. Measure risk.
4. Execute revisions and adjustments when risk measures are out of line.

Risk exposures of a portfolio or a position should be measured periodically. Risk exposures of a position that involves derivative securities are of particular interest. We examine in great detail risk factors in a derivative security later in this reading.

Risk management is not just about reducing risk and hedging. Instead, it is a process of managing risk. Risk management is about risk modification. When risks are priced below a certain benchmark determined by pricing models, managers may increase the amount of risk in a position or a transaction. Similarly, when risks are priced above a certain benchmark, managers should reduce the risk level in a position or a transaction.

Risk governance is a set of policies, standards, and rules based on which risk management process is conducted. Top management in a company is responsible for risk governance. Top management needs to determine the structure of risk governance: whether the risk management process should be conducted centralized or decentralized.

LOS 31b: Evaluate strengths and weaknesses of a company's risk management process. Vol 5, pp 140–151

There are costs and benefits for both centralized and decentralized forms of risk management. Under the centralized risk management structure, a single risk management group oversees all risk factors of the whole enterprise. The risk management group is close to the top management and can easily communicate with the top management. It potentially achieves economy of scale. It can improve efficiency by monitoring risk factors only after they are netted among potential multiple subsidiaries within the same firm. In a firm with multiple subsidiaries, the overall risk of the firm is less than the sum of risks of individual subsidiaries because of diversification effect across different divisions of the firm. A key benefit of the centralized structure is that it allows the top management to fully understand the overall risk of the enterprise. However, a decentralized structure allows the risk management team to be closer to the risk exposure which risk management team attempts to hedge. Being closer to the risk exposure is likely to provide a better understanding of the risk exposure and consequently a more effective hedge at the decentralized level.

An enterprise risk management (ERM) system includes the following steps:

1. Identify all risk factors to which the company is exposed.
2. Quantify each risk factor's size in monetary terms.
3. Input the monetary risk exposures to compute the overall risk and contribution of each risk factor.
4. Report the overall risk to the top management, which determines capital allocations, risk limits, and risk management policies.
5. Monitor compliance with policies and risk limits.

LESSON 2: IDENTIFYING RISK

Candidates should master the following concepts:

1. Identify risk factors in an enterprise;
2. Understand financial risk and non-financial risk:
   - Financial risk includes market risk, interest rate risk, exchange rate risk, equity price risk, commodity price risk, credit risk, liquidity risk, and others;
   - Non-financial risk includes account risk, tax risk, legal risk, regulatory risk, settlement risk, model risk, operation risk, and others;

RISK IDENTIFICATION

LOS 31d: Evaluate a company's or a portfolio's exposures to financial and non-financial risk factors. Vol 5, pp 140–151

The first key step in the risk management process is to identify all risk factors to which the firm is exposed. There are two major categories of risk factors. Financial risks are risk factors derived from the external financial markets. Non-financial risks are all other risk factors. Financial risks include, but are not limited to, risk factors such as interest rate risk, exchange rate risk, equity price risk, commodity price risk, credit risk, and liquidity risk. Non-financial risks include, but are not limited to, risk factors such as accounting risk, operation risk, model risk, settlement risk, risks associated with regulations, and changes in regulations, legal systems, and taxes.

Example 2-1

Convenience Products, Inc. is a manufacturer of construction material. It produces industry-use sealants and insulation foams. Headquartered in St. Louis, Missouri, the firm has expanded its product market from local Midwest U.S. to coast-to-coast U.S., and lately, to central America, Australia, Asia, and Europe. Convenience Products buys raw material from its suppliers and sells its final products to customers for cash or on credit. Additionally, the firm's stocks are traded on the NASDAQ and its debt is mostly bank notes.

Identify *all* risk factors to which the firm is exposed.

Solution:

The firm is exposed to both financial risk and non-financial risk.

Financial risk includes:

- Interest rate risk: The firm borrows from banks.
- Exchange rate risk: The firm makes sales overseas and collects foreign currencies.
- Equity price risk: The firm's stock is traded on the NASDAQ and is exposed to stock market risk.
- Commodity price risk: The firm buys raw material from local markets.
- Credit risk: The firm extends credits to its customers and may fail to collect from its customers.
- Liquidity risk: the firm may over-stock its inventory and may not be able to quickly convert its inventory into cash to meet its short-term liquidity needs.

Non-financial risk includes:

- Operation risk: The firm's production process may be interrupted by factors beyond control, such as tornados or flooding in the Midwest U.S.
- Regulation risk: The government may limit or eliminate productions for increased environmental concerns.

Financial Risk

We examine each type of risk in detail below. First we investigate financial risks.

Market Risk

Market risk includes risk factors that are associated with interest rates, exchange rates, stock pricings, and commodity prices. These risks are sourced from the relation between supply and demand dynamics in different markets. For example, the uncertainty in the value of a foreign currency such as the euro to an American investor is due to dynamic changes in supply and demand for the euro in the currency market.

Credit Risk

Credit risk includes default risk, but it also incorporates uncertainties in credit quality change of a firm. It is associated with one party's failure to make a promised payment to another party. Credit risk is of particular importance in the over-the-counter derivative markets because most likely, there are no third-party guarantees on these derivative transactions. Consequently, each party is exposed to the credit risk of the other counterparty.

Liquidity Risk

Liquidity risk is the risk of an asset that cannot be sold promptly without a significant discount due to the market's inability to find a counterparty to complete the transaction. The U.S. equity market is considered liquid. However, the level of liquidity varies significantly across different stocks. In general, large cap stocks enjoy much better liquidity than small cap stocks. Small cap stocks carry much more liquidity risk than large cap stocks. Liquidity on the same asset may also change over time. During the Great Financial Crisis in 2008–2009, many corporate securities (stocks and bonds) lost much of their liquidity because investors had so much fear holding corporate stocks and bonds due to potential default risks associated with these securities. After the crisis, liquidity risk became much less pronounced for most stocks and bonds. One measure of liquidity risk for traded assets is the difference between the ask price and bid price in a price quote, called bid-ask spread. A wide bid-ask spread is often associated with low liquidity and high liquidity risk. Other measures of liquidity risk include the Amihud's (2002) illiquidity ratio and trading volume. A high trading volume is associated with high liquidity and low liquidity risk.

Non-Financial Risk

Now we turn to non-financial risks.

Operational Risk

Operational risk (operation risk) is the loss from failure of the firm's system, procedure, or other external events. Operation risk includes risk factors such as computer failure, which has previously happened even in the U.S. stock exchanges, when trading has to be halted because of failed computer systems. Operation risk also includes natural disasters, such as hurricanes, earthquakes, and flooding. Some operation risks can be hedged or eliminated by insurance policies. However, many other types of operation risks cannot be easily eliminated.

Model Risk

Model risk arises when an incorrect financial model is applied to measure risk and/or value. For example, in derivative security pricing, investors often use the 1996 Nobel Prize winner, the Black-Scholes-Merton option pricing model, to value options. However, options markets do not satisfy many model assumptions specified in the Black-Scholes-Merton model, making the model mis-specified in the context of options markets in reality. If investors naively believe in the Black-Scholes-Merton model price without making any adjustments, they are subject to model risk.

Settlement Risk

Settlement risk is the cash flow uncertainty in a transaction where one party expects payment from another party but the other party is declaring bankruptcy. Such a situation arises in a spot market transaction as well as in a derivative market transaction. Given that exchange traded securities, especially derivative securities, generally have clearing corporations behind all trades, marginal accounts protect parties from both sides of the transaction from settlement risk. In OTC markets, settlement risk can be significant. One good way to reduce settlement risk is to net cash flows so that only the difference in payments remains payable from one party to the other party. Another way to reduce settlement risk is to perform frequent mark-to-market on OTC derivative positions so that the size of the loss, if any, is substantially reduced.

Regulatory Risk

Regulatory risk is the uncertainty associated with a transaction due to potential change in regulations. Governments across different countries impose trading rules to transaction in financial markets. The rules may change over time. New rules may be added. Existing rules may be modified or removed. All these changes create regulatory risk. Regulatory risk varies significantly over time and across different countries.

Legal/Contract Risk

Legal/contract risk is the risk of one counterparty in a legally binding contract failing to perform according to the contract, and the legal system fails to enforce the contract. In the OTC derivative markets, a derivative contract may be negotiated between a dealer and a counterparty. However, either the dealer or the counterparty may fail to carry out obligations based on the derivative contract. Security law may not fully enforce the derivative contract based on its original terms. Legal/contract risk exists in financial markets.

Tax Risk

Tax risk is the uncertainty associated with tax laws. Tax laws can be extremely complex, and are often time varying. Sometimes, tax laws are subject to interpretation, and can be inconsistent and confusing. The risk associated with change of tax laws is tax risk.

Accounting Risk

Accounting risk is the risk of correctly and accurately recording transactions based on the current accounting standards. Law requires that a firm's transactions and performance be accurately documented in accounting statements. However, accounting treatment for some transactions, such as derivative use and derivative contracts, can raise confusion. When a firm incorrectly reports financial statements, the firm needs to subsequently restate its financials, which sends a negative signal to the market because investors may believe that the firm had an intention to hide information.

Sovereign and Political Risks

Sovereign risk is a type of credit risk when the borrower is a government. Note that default on a loan depends on both the willingness to pay and the ability to pay. A government body may have the ability to pay, but not the willingness to pay, possibly resulting in a default, which generates sovereign risk. Political risk is the risk associated with changes in the political environment.

Other Risks

ESG risk is risk associated with environmental, social, and governance factors. Netting risk is a risk factor due to the asymmetric nature of performance reward and penalty. In a multi-strategy multi-manager environment, there can be a situation where the overall performance of the firm across multiple managers is flat, but some managers earn performance incentive bonuses due to positive performance, while no penalty is imposed on managers who deliver inferior performance. To the extreme, a manager could hold a long position and a short position on the same underlying risky asset. At the end of a performance evaluation period, one position beats a benchmark and the other position lags the benchmark. Even though the manager's overall performance is net zero, he might get rewarded for the first position and not penalized for the second position. This very naive and simple example demonstrates performance netting risk.

LESSON 3: MEASURING RISK: VALUE AT RISK (VAR)

Candidates should master the following concepts:

- Measures of market risk: volatility, beta, duration, delta, and others;

Understand VAR. It's a key concept in this reading:

- Understand three methods to compute VAR: analytical method, historical method, and Monte Carlo simulation method;

RISK MEASUREMENT

We now have identified many risk factors in ERM (enterprise risk management). We need to quantify the magnitude of the risk factors so that we can effectively manage these risk factors. We introduce a key concept in this section. It's called Value at Risk (VAR), which is a widely accepted term in risk management in the finance industry, especially in portfolio management, among others.

Measuring Market Risk

Note that market risk refers to risks in interest rates, exchange rates, equity prices, and commodity prices.

A commonly used measure of risk is called volatility. The accurate reference of volatility is the annualized asset return standard deviation. Note that the volatility is the standard deviation of asset returns, and not asset prices. If it were for prices, then assets with high prices generally would inherently have higher price volatility than assets with low prices. Also note that the return standard deviation is annualized. The notation for volatility is the Greek letter sigma (σ). It measures the total risk of an asset or a portfolio.

In the CAPM framework, we model the returns of a security using a single-factor model and conclude that return on any security is determined by the return on the market index. The amount of systematic risk a security carries is measured by beta, which is the sensitivity of security return with respect to market index return.

Using a similar sensitivity measure, a bond duration measures the amount of interest rate risk a bond carries. It is the sensitivity of the price of a bond with respect to a small change in bond yield. Similarly, an option delta measures the rate of option price change with respect to a small change in the underlying asset price. Both bond duration and option delta provide the first order approximation of risk, measured by the rate of change of the asset price with respect to a change in the underlying risk factor (bond yield and underlying asset price).

To be more accurate in measuring price risk, second-order measures are often used. Bond convexity captures how bond duration changes as bond yield changes. Option gamma captures how option delta changes as underlying asset price changes. Both measures allow an investor to better understand the dynamics of bond price and option price changes with respect to underlying risk factor (bond yield and underlying asset price) changes.

An option price can be viewed as a multivariate function. It is determined by multiple risk factors, such as the risk-free interest rate, stock return volatility, as well as passage of time. The rate of change in option price with respect to change in risk-free interest rate is called rho. The rate of change in option price with respect to change in stock return volatility (sigma) is called vega. The rate of change in option price with respect to change in remaining time to option maturity is called theta.

Sigma, beta, duration, convexity, delta, gamma, vega, rho, and theta are all measures of risk.

LOS 31e: Calculate and interpret value at risk (VAR) and explain its role in measuring overall and individual position market risk. Vol 5, pp 152–153

LOS 31f: Compare the analytical (variance–covariance), historical, and Monte Carlo methods for estimating VAR and discuss the advantages and disadvantages of each. Vol 5, pp 155–168

Value at Risk (VAR)

Value at Risk (VAR) is the minimum amount of money we expect to lose in a given reporting period with a given level of probability. The interpretation of VAR is important. Note that VAR has a probability dimension and a time dimension. For a given probability and a given reporting time period, the minimum amount of loss is what the VAR measure attempts to describe. The true loss, based on the same given level of probability, is expected to be larger than the VAR amount because the VAR amount is the minimum level of loss. Exhibit 3-1 best describes the VAR concept.

Exhibit 3-1: Value at Risk (VAR)

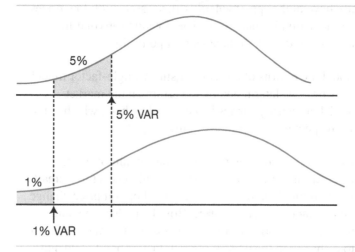

Exhibit 3-1 assumes that the distribution of returns over the next time period follow a normal specification. VAR captures the action at the lower tail (left tail). When the left tail is 5 percent, there is a 5 percent probability that the return in the next time period is less than a critical point, which defines the 5 percent VAR. Consistent with the definition of VAR, the probability of losing [5 percent VAR] or more is 5 percent.

Similarly, Exhibit 3-1 plots 1 percent VAR in the lower panel of the figure. Note that 1 percent VAR is always smaller than 5 percent VAR by logic, simply because how VAR is defined. Take 5 percent VAR as −20 percent for example, if there is a 5 percent probability that we lose 20 percent or more in the next time period, then the loss we suffer must be worse than −20 percent (e.g., −27 percent) with 1 percent probability.

The following table presents the frequency distribution of annual returns of the S&P 500 Index over 1825–2010. Based on this empirical distribution, we can apply the VAR concept and ask some questions related to VAR.

Range of Stock Returns	Probability
−50% to −40%	0.5%
−40% to −30%	1.1%
−30% to −20%	3.2%
−20% to −10%	9.1%
−10% to 0%	15.6%
0% to 10%	24.2%
10% to 20%	19.9%
20% to 30%	12.9%
30% to 40%	8.1%
40% to 50%	2.7%
50% to 60%	2.7%

What is the 5 percent VAR? We need to find the cumulative distribution function from the left. Essentially we need to find the fifth percentile. Because of the discreteness of the distribution, we have 4.8 percent of all observations below −20 percent and 13.9 percent of distributions below −10 percent. If we round 4.8 percent to 5.0 percent, we state that there is a 5 percent probability that the minimum loss in a given year is −20 percent. Alternatively, we can state that once out of 20 years (5 percent), we expect a loss of −20 percent or more. Clearly, the empirical distribution supports the statement.

Similarly, we can find 0.5 percent VAR, which is −40 percent. We state that there is a 0.5 percent probability that the minimum loss in a given year is −40 percent. Alternatively, we can state that once out of 200 years (0.5 percent) we expect a loss of −40 percent or more.

The method we have applied is based on historical (empirical) data. It's called the historical method, or the historical simulation method. The advantage of this method is that the results are based on historical performance of the security in the past and that the calculation is not subject to any return distribution assumptions. The historical method is an example of a nonparametric method. However, the weakness of the method is that it implicitly assumes that the future performance is a repetition of the past performance, which is inappropriate.

Example 3-1

The following are the 30 worst of 100 weekly returns of Facebook ending September 22, 2014.

−0.1075	−0.0469	−0.0346
−0.0930	−0.0446	−0.0345
−0.0739	−0.0435	−0.0329
−0.0649	−0.0423	−0.0298
−0.0609	−0.0420	−0.0283
−0.0576	−0.0419	−0.0247
−0.0574	−0.0397	−0.0209
−0.0567	−0.0378	−0.0205
−0.0543	−0.0376	−0.0205
−0.0533	−0.0369	−0.0194

Based on the realized weekly returns, **compute** the 5 percent VAR and 1 percent VAR. Note that the returns have been sorted in an increasing order.

Solution:

The fifth percentile of the observations define the 5 percent VAR. In this case, there are exactly 100 observations. The 5 percent VAR is the 5th observation, which is −0.0609. We conclude that there is a 5 percent probability that a weekly loss is a loss of 6.09 percent or more. Similarly, there is a 1 percent probability that a weekly loss is a loss of 10.75 percent or more.

Instead of using this historical method, as we described above, a more industry standard method is the analytical or variance-covariance method. In this method, we explicitly assume that asset returns are normally distributed. Consequently, returns on a portfolio of assets whose returns are individually normally distributed also follow a normal distribution.

We use a numerical example to demonstrate applications of the analytical method to compute VAR. Consider an investor who holds Stock A and Stock B. The portfolio weights are 70 percent in A and 30 percent in B. Stock A carries an expected annual return of 15 percent and an annual return standard 48 percent. Stock B carries an expected annual return of 18 percent and an annual return standard 66 percent. The correlation between returns of Stock A and Stock B is 0.29. **Compute** the 5 percent annual VAR.

The following table summarizes our known information.

	Stock A	Stock B	Portfolio
Portfolio weight	0.70	0.30	1.00
Expected return	0.15	0.18	15.90%
Standard deviation	0.48	0.66	43.67%
Correlation	0.29		

Based on portfolio theory, we have the following results:

$$r_P = w_1 r_1 + w_2 r_2$$
$$= 0.70 \times 0.15 + 0.30 \times 0.18$$
$$= 15.90\%$$

$$\sigma_P^2 = w_1^2 \sigma_1^2 + w_2^2 \sigma_2^2 + 2w_1 w_2 \rho \sigma_1 \sigma_2$$
$$= 0.70^2 \times 0.48^2 + 0.30^2 \times 0.66^2 + 2 \times 0.70 \times 0.30 \times 0.29 \times 0.48 \times 0.66$$
$$= 0.190686$$

$$\sigma_P = 43.67\%$$

The portfolio has an expected annual return of 15.90 percent and an annualized return standard deviation of 43.67 percent. To compute the 5 percent annual VAR, we examine the following Exhibit 3-2.

Exhibit 3-2: Percent Annual Value at Risk (VAR)

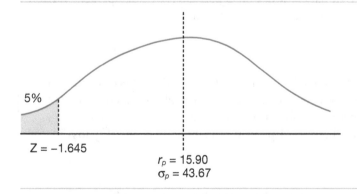

5%

$Z = -1.645$

$r_p = 15.90$
$\sigma_p = 43.67$

Given a 5 percent lower tail, we look up the standard normal table to find the corresponding Z-score to be −1.645. We have:

$$-1.645 = \frac{VAR_{5\%} - 0.1590}{0.4367}$$
$$VAR_{5\%} = -55.94\%$$

We conclude the 5 percent annual VAR to be −55.94 percent. There is a 5 percent chance that we lose at least 55.94 percent of the investment in the next year. Clearly this investment is very risky.

Example 3-2

A portfolio manager is holding positions in a U.S. stock index and a Latin American stock index. The characteristics of the indices and asset allocation weights are listed below.

	U.S. Index	Latin American Index	Portfolio
Portfolio weight	0.60	0.40	1.00
Expected return	0.12	0.20	??
Standard deviation	0.15	0.37	??
Correlation	0.57		

Compute the following:

i.   A 5 percent annual VAR.

ii.   A 1 percent annual VAR.

iii. A 5 percent monthly VAR.

iv.   A 1 percent monthly VAR.

Solutions:

i. We first compute the portfolio expected return and return standard deviation.

$$r_P = w_1 r_1 + w_2 r_2$$
$$= 0.60 \times 0.12 + 0.40 \times 0.20$$
$$= 15.20\%$$

$$\sigma_p^2 = w_1^2 \sigma_1^2 + w_2^2 \sigma_2^2 + 2 w_1 w_2 \rho \sigma_1 \sigma_2$$
$$= 0.60^2 \times 0.15^2 + 0.40^2 \times 0.37^2 + 2 \times 0.60 \times 0.40 \times 0.57 \times 0.15 \times 0.37$$
$$= 0.045189$$

$$\sigma_\rho = 21.26\%$$

A 5 percent annual VAR:

$$-1.645 = \frac{VAR_{5\% \text{ annual}} - 0.1520}{0.2126}$$
$$VAR_{5\% \text{ annual}} = -19.77\%$$

ii. A 1 percent annual VAR:

$$-2.326 = \frac{VAR_{1\% \text{annual}} - 0.1520}{0.2126}$$
$$VAR_{1\% \text{ annual}} = -34.25\%$$

iii. A 5 percent monthly VAR:

$$-1.645 = \frac{VAR_{5\% \text{ monthly}} - 0.1520/12}{0.2126/\sqrt{12}}$$
$$VAR_{5\% \text{ monthly}} = -8.837\%$$

iv. A 1 percent monthly VAR:

$$-2.326 = \frac{VAR_{1\% \text{ monthly}} - 0.1520/12}{0.2126/\sqrt{12}}$$
$$VAR_{1\% \text{ monthly}} = -13.01\%$$

For the same time horizon, we observe that 1 percent VAR is smaller than 5 percent VAR, which matches our intuition and logic. For the same level of probability, 1 percent or 5 percent, the annual VAR is smaller than the monthly VAR.

LOS 31g: Discuss advantages and limitations of VAR and its extensions, including cash flow at risk, earnings at risk, and tail value at risk.
Vol 5, pp 168–170

The analytical method is simple and easy to use, as we demonstrate in the above examples. However, the trouble is that the normality assumptions generally do not hold. It is particularly true when there are options in a portfolio. Options can significantly change the payoff and risk profile of a portfolio in such a way that the distribution of returns is truncated on either the upside (such as in a covered call) or downside (such as in a protective put) or both (such as in an option collar). In such a situation, we should use the delta-normal method, where we analyze the risk exposure of a portfolio with options using a small change in the underlying stock price. In the analysis, we may include both option delta and option gamma to compute gains and/or losses in the overall portfolio with options due to a small change in the underlying stock price.

Additionally, even without the presence of options, historical stock returns and stock index returns are known to display skewness and kurtosis. Skewness measures the degree to which a distribution is asymmetric around the mean. Kurtosis measures the amount of fat tails shown in a distribution. Historically, we observe negative skewness, meaning that there are more negative extreme returns than positive extreme returns. We also observe excess kurtosis, meaning there are more extreme events than implied by a normal distribution specification. Both negative skewness and excess kurtosis are violations of normality assumption. When we apply the analytical method (variance-covariance method) to compute VAR, we should fully understand the model assumptions. Our results are valid only to the extent that our assumptions are valid.

There is also diversification effect in VAR. Consider a firm with multiple lines of business or multiple divisions. Each division has its own stand-alone VAR. However, when we consider the overall VAR of the firm, it is not simply the sum of individual divisional VARs. There are often diversification benefits so that the firm's overall VAR is less than the sum of individual divisional VARs.

Even though VAR is a popular measure of risk, it has its limitations. (1) VAR does not estimate risk over a long time horizon where extreme events are more likely to present; (2) VAR does not directly consider impact of liquidity of a portfolio or a position; and (3) historical price and return performance may not accurately predict future price and return movements. Consequently, VAR calculations based on historical method may not be accurate.

The third approach to compute VAR is based on Monte Carlo simulation. Based on an assumed distribution of risk factors, Monte Carlo simulation generates random realizations of prices or returns based on which VAR is computed. Note that this method uses a probability distribution of each risk factor and generates outcomes based on the distribution of these risk factors. It clearly allows existence of multiple risk factors in a model without added assumptions of joint distributions of these risk factors. The Monte Carlo simulation method has the advantage over the analytical (variance-covariance) method in that the Monte Carlo simulation method can be applied when functional forms of probability distributions of risk factors are not directly available, or even if they are available, they are extremely complex and are difficult to produce an analytical solution.

Even though VAR has been the industry standard for measuring risk exposures in recent years, VAR measure and its methods have their limitations.

1. VAR can be difficult to estimate and different methods may yield different VAR values.
2. VAR considers only the downside risk and fails to incorporate upside benefits.
3. VAR calculation is often based on distributional assumptions, which may not be valid.

Backtesting is one effective way to verify that the computed VAR is reasonably accurate. In this context, backtesting involves recording the number of occurrences where the ex-post realized losses exceed the VAR threshold and compare the percentage of such occurrences against the VAR level. For example, if the 5 percent weekly VAR is $17 million for a portfolio over a week, over a 200-week period, we should observe about 10 (5 percent of 200) weeks where the weekly loss is greater than $17 million. If during the 200-week period, the number of weeks where weekly losses are greater than $17 million is significantly different from 10, we have evidence against that the 5 percent weekly VAR is $17 million. If backtesting consistently produces satisfactory results, we should have confidence in the VAR estimate.

IVAR stands for incremental VAR. It's the difference between the VAR of a portfolio including a specific asset and the VAR of the same portfolio without the specific asset. IVAR measures the incremental impact in VAR by including an asset in a portfolio.

TVAR stands for tail VAR. It's the conditional tail expectation. It is defined as the VAR plus the expected loss in excess of VAR conditional on such loss occurring. Unlike VAR, which measures the minimum amount of loss, TVAR measures the expected size of loss conditional on the loss being greater than VAR.

LESSON 4: MEASURING RISK: VAR EXTENSIONS AND STRESS TESTING

Candidates should master the following concept:

- Understand stress testing and factor push.

LOS 31h: Compare alternative types of stress testing and discuss advantages and disadvantages of each. Vol 5, pp 170–172

Stress Testing

In addition to VaR, risk managers also use stress testing to gauge the amount of risk present in a portfolio or a firm. Unlike VaR, which measures losses due to risk exposures under normal market conditions, stress testing attempts to identify unusual situations that can lead to significant losses. Stress testing includes two approaches: scenario analysis and stressing models.

Scenario Analysis

Scenario analysis examines the value of a portfolio under different extreme conditions, for example, large interest rate movements or large equity price shocks. Some stylized scenarios, listed here, are candidates under which condition the value of a portfolio is examined for risk management purposes.

- Stock index levels change by 10 percent in either a positive or negative direction;
- Option implied volatility of stock returns change by 30 percent;
- A 100 basis-point parallel shift in yield curve;
- Value of major currencies changes by 10 percent and value of other currencies changes by 20 percent;
- Asset liquidity decreases significantly.

Alternatively, scenario analysis may also examine the value of a portfolio under conditions of actual extreme events that occurred in the past. Such events may include the Black Friday of October 19, 1987, the terrorist attack of September 11, 2001, or the bankruptcy of Lehman Brothers during the financial crisis in September 2008. Analysis of portfolio performance under these extreme events helps risk managers to gauge the impact of extreme events on portfolio value.

LOS 31m: Demonstrate the use of VAR and stress testing in setting capital requirements. Vol 5, pp 171–172

Stressing Models

Stressing models are another way to perform stress tests. The challenge in the stressing model is that the risk manager needs to build a mathematical model to value the portfolio of securities. Then the risk manager performs something called factor push, which is a process of pushing the risk factor(s) in the model to produce the worst case scenario of the value of the portfolio. This process allows risk managers and portfolio managers to better understand the risk embedded in a portfolio as well as its impact on portfolio value and returns.

Stress testing provides a complementary dimension to VaR measures and helps portfolio managers to be more effective in portfolio risk management.

LESSON 5: MEASURING RISK: CREDIT RISK

Candidates should master the following concepts:

- Understand credit risk
- Understand risk budgeting

LOS 31i: Evaluate the credit risk of an investment position, including forward contract, swap, and option positions. Vol 5, pp 172–179

Credit Risk

Credit risk is an important source of risk. It often appears in a bond portfolio or a portfolio with derivatives, especially OTC derivatives. Credit risk arises when one party is subject to losses if its counterparty fails to deliver payment or carry out a contract due to a default. Credit risk has two important dimensions: the likelihood of default and the amount of loss due to a default given that a default occurs. The first term, the likelihood of default, is a probability. However, just because a counterparty has a higher probability to default does not necessarily imply that the counterparty has a higher credit risk. The reason is that we should also consider the expected magnitude of loss given a default occurs. In a bond setting, it is the recovery rate in case of a bond default.

There are two types of credit risk: current credit risk and potential credit risk. They are related to the timing of a credit event. Current credit risk is also known as jump-to-default risk. It is the risk of ongoing default or a pending default that will occur in the immediate future. For example, a firm is in default of its bonds. A portfolio manager holding these bonds is subject to current credit risk of the bonds. Alternatively, consider the following example of current credit risk. A buyer of an OTC option intends to exercise her options against the option writer tomorrow. However, it is clear that the option writer is unable to fulfill the option exercise due to financial constraints. Consequently, the option buyer is exposed to current credit risk in the option position.

Potential credit risk is risk of possible default in the future. In our bond example, if the issuer continues to make regular coupon payments, the bond does not have current credit risk. However, over time, the firm's financial strength may change and the firm may default in the future. Bondholders are exposed to potential credit risk and not current credit risk in this case.

Another type of credit risk can be viewed as a hybrid of current credit risk and potential credit risk. It is the risk to a portfolio manager that a counterparty defaults on a current debt obligation to a third-party creditor. Note that in this case, the counterparty does not directly default on the obligation to the portfolio manager. Instead, it defaults on a third party. However, the cross-default provision included in the debt or derivative contract triggers the portfolio manger's claim against the counterparty as long as the counterparty defaults on any of its obligations with any of its creditors. The cross-default provision protects creditors and reduces credit risk because in case of a default, the creditor would like to react as soon as possible to take action to recover assets before they are taken by other creditors.

Credit VAR is also called default VAR or credit at risk. It is a measure of credit risk. The concept is similar to that of VAR. It measures the minimum amount of loss due to credit risk over a reporting period with a given probability. A 5 percent annual credit VAR of $1 million states that there is a 5 percent chance that we lose more than $1 million due to defaults in the next year. Alternatively, we can state that we are 95 percent confident that the amount of loss due to default will be less than $1 million in the next year.

Another point that is worth attention is that credit risk rises in up markets. In a derivative market setting, due to the zero-sum game nature of derivative securities, in down markets, the firm's position is at the risk of default. Consequently, the firm's counterparty carries the firm's default risk. The firm does not have the counterparty's (current) credit risk. In up markets, the firm's derivative contracts are assets, such as an in-the-money option, while the counterparties hold liabilities. In this case, the firm carries the counterparties' credit risk because the counterparties may default on the liabilities. So the credit VAR is located in the upper tail of the firm's return distribution while the traditional VAR is located in the lower tail of the firm's return distribution.

Stocks of a Firm with Bonds Subject to Default Risk

An important insight in corporate finance and option theory casts a different view of stocks in a levered firm whose bonds are subject to default risk. Stocks in a levered firm can be viewed as a call option on the firm's assets.

Consider a levered firm. For simplicity, we assume the firm's bond is a zero coupon bond with a face value of F. The current market value of the bond is B_0. The value of the firm's assets is A_0. Consequently, the value of the firm's equity (stock) S_0 is the difference between the value of the firm's assets and its bonds. We have:

$$S_0 = A_0 - B_0$$

At the bond's expiration, what is the value of the firm's stock and what is the value of the firm's bonds? Note that if the value of the firm is less than the face value of the firm's bonds, the firm is bankrupted; the bondholders take over the firm, and the stockholders get a zero residual value. Also note that if the value of the firm is greater than the face value of the firm's bonds, the bondholders are paid off by the face value of the bonds; the stockholders get a positive residual value after the bondholders are paid off. We have:

$$B_T = \min(A_T, F)$$
$$S_T = \max(A_T - F, 0)$$

A careful examination of the equation of the stock value reminds us the terminal value of a call option on a share of stock at expiration:

$$c_T = \max(S_T - X, 0)$$

where: c is the value of the call option; S is the value of the stock, and X is the option's exercise price.

We conclude that the stock on a levered firm can be viewed as a call option on the firm's assets, where the call option's exercise price is the face value of the firm's debt. We apply the put-call parity relation of European-style options to this particular setting:

$$S_0 + p = PV(X) + c$$
$$A_0 + p = PV(F) + S_0$$

Transforming the second equation, we have:

$$A_0 = S_0 + PV(F) - p$$

Comparing the above equation with:

$$A_0 = S_0 + B_0$$

We have:

$$S_0 = c$$
$$B_0 = PV(F) - p$$

The stockholders of a levered firm have a call option on the firm's assets. Consequently, they have limited liability. They can walk away without any obligations in case the firm is bankrupted. The loss of the bankruptcy is taken by bondholders of the firm. The above equation clearly states that the bondholders have effectively written a put option to the firm, allowing the firm to replace the bankrupted firm with the bond's face value at bond maturity in case of bankruptcy.

CFA candidates should carefully examine these relations and fully understand the insight on corporate securities (stocks and bonds) cased in option theory framework. To summarize, when investors buy stocks, they buy a call option on the firm's assets; when investors buy bonds, they sell a put option on the firm's assets to the firm.

Credit Risk of Forward Contracts

In a forward contract, both the long party and the short party are exposed to the credit risk of the other party during the life of the forward contract. The main reason of existence of credit risk in a forward contract is that a position in a forward contract is generally not marked-to-market, as a position in a futures contract. Gains or losses may accumulate over time such that credit risk becomes significant.

Consider the following simple example. The spot gold price is $1,200 per ounce and one-year risk-free rate is 4 percent. Assuming that there is no storage cost and no convenience, the one-year forward price should be:

$$F = 1,200 \times 1.04 = \$1,248 \text{ per ounce}$$

Now, three months later, the spot price becomes $1,180. What's the value of the forward contract to the long party? Well, the value to the long is the difference in present value of cash inflow and cash outflow:

$$V = 1,180 - \frac{1,248}{1.04^{0.75}} = -\$31.82 \text{ per ounce}$$

So the value to the long party is −$31.82 per ounce. Note that the long party of the forward contract bets the forward/spot price to increase. In this case, the spot price decreased and the long party has made a wrong bet. The long party loses and the short party gains.

Which party bears the credit risk? The answer is the short party. The short party bears the credit risk of the long party because the long party may default on the payment of its liabilities. The risk is a potential credit risk because no payment is currently due.

Example 5-1

Three months ago, a portfolio manager sold a one-year forward contract on a stock index for $388. The current stock index level is at $400. The stock index carries a continuously compounded dividend yield of 2.7 percent. The current continuously compounded risk-free rate is 4.2 percent.

Analyze credit risk *and* the amount of potential credit loss in the following forward contract.

Solution:

We first compute the value of the forward contract. Then we analyze which party carries credit risk of the forward contract at this moment.

Today's forward price is determined by the cost of carry model:

$$F_t = S_t e^{(r-\delta)(T-t)}$$

The value of a *long* forward contract is:

$$
\begin{aligned}
V_t &= PV[F_t - F_0] \\
&= [F_t - F_0]e^{-r(T-t)} \\
&= [S_t e^{(r-\delta)(T-t)} - F_0]e^{-r(T-t)} \\
&= S_t e^{-\delta(T-t)} - F_0 e^{-r(T-t)}
\end{aligned}
$$

The value of a *short* forward contract is:

$$
\begin{aligned}
V_{t,short} &= -[S_t e^{-\delta(T-t)} - F_0 e^{-r(T-t)}] \\
&= -[400e^{-0.07(0.75)} - 388e^{-0.042(0.75)}] \\
&= -\$16.0130
\end{aligned}
$$

The value of the short party (the manager) is −\$16.0130 per unit of the stock index. Because the value is negative, the manager is carrying a liability at this point in time. So the long party, the manager's counterparty, carries the credit risk of the manager at this time. Of course, as time moves on and as the stock index value changes, things can turn around and the manger can carry credit risk of the counterparty.

Credit Risk of Swap Contracts

A swap contract can be viewed as a portfolio of similar forward contracts. Consequently, the issues of credit risk associated with a forward contract apply to swap contracts. The difference is that in a swap contract, there are multiple payments, where in a forward contract, there is only one payment. The party carrying the credit risk is the party that holds a positive value of the swap. The value of the swap is the present value of its cash inflows minus the present value of cash outflows.

The amount of credit risk varies significantly over the life of a swap contract. For an interest rate swap and an equity swap, potential credit risk is highest during the middle period of the swap's life. For a currency swap, potential credit risk is highest between the middle period and the end of the swap's life because notional principals are exchanged at the tenor of a currency swap.

Example 5-2

In a vanilla interest rate swap with semi-annual payments, there are the last two payments left, one in four months and one in 10 months. The swap fixed rate is 4.2 percent and the upcoming floating-rate payment is based on 3.8 percent. A portfolio manager is on the pay-floating and receive-fixed side of the swap. Using the 30-day month and 360-day year day count, the current term structure of interest rates is:

60-day rate:	5.0%
120-day rate:	5.1%
180-day rate:	5.2%
240-day rate:	5.3%
300-day rate:	5.4%
360-day rate:	5.5%

Analyze credit risk *and* the amount of potential credit loss in the swap contract.

Solution:

We first compute the value of the swap contract to the portfolio manager. Then we analyze which party carries credit risk of the swap contract at this moment.

The value of the fixed-rate payments:

$$V_{\text{Fixed rate}} = \frac{0.021}{1 + 0.051 \times \frac{120}{360}} + \frac{1.021}{1 + 0.054 \times \frac{300}{360}} = 0.9977$$

The value of the floating-rate payments:

$$V_{\text{Floating rate}} = \frac{1.019}{1 + 0.051 \times \frac{120}{360}} = 1.0020$$

Note that we need to use only 120-day rate and 300-day rate. All other rates are distractors.

The manager is on the pay-floating and receive-fixed side. So his position value is:

$$V_{\text{Pay floating and receive fixed}} = V_{\text{Fixed rate}} - V_{\text{Floating rate}}$$
$$= 0.9977 - 1.0020$$
$$= -\$0.0043$$

The value of the manager's position is −$0.0043 per $1 of notional principal. Because the value is negative, the manager is carrying a liability at this point in time. The manager's counterparty carries the credit risk of the manager at this time. Of course, as time moves on and as interest rates change, things can turn around and the manger can carry credit risk of the counterparty.

Credit Risk of Option Contracts

Unlike forward contracts and swap contracts, where both the long and short parties are subject to the credit risk of the other party, in an option contract, credit risk applies to only option buyers. Option buyers hold an asset and they don't have any liabilities from the long option position. Consequently, option sellers do not carry any credit risk of option buyers. However, option sellers hold a liability due to the short option position. Option sellers may default on option buyer's exercise of options. Consequently, option buyers carry credit risk of option sellers.

Consider an example where an option writer sells a put option to an option buyer for $5. The option buyer pays $5 for the put option to the option seller. Now at this moment, the option buyer carries potential credit risk from the option seller. If the option seller defaults now, the option buyer suffers a credit loss of $5. Of course, as time goes by, stock price and many other market conditions will change, and the size of credit risk and potential credit loss the long party may suffer also changes.

Example 5-3

An option dealer has written a put option on a stock index for $48 to an investor. Due to the recent decrease in stock return volatility, the value of the put option is now $27.

Analyze credit risk *and* the amount of potential credit loss in the option contract.

Solution:

The investor paid $48 for the put option. Now the put option is worth $27. The investor lost $21 (on a per share basis). However, that's not the point. The investor holds a put option. When she intends to exercise the put option against the dealer, the dealer may default and the dealer may not be able to fulfill the put exercise. So, clearly, the investor is exposed to the credit risk of the dealer. The amount of potential credit loss at this moment is $27.

Liquidity Risk and Nonfinancial Risks

Liquidity risk has become an increasingly important risk factor in today's financial markets. An important assumption of VAR calculation is that markets are liquid and assets can be traded without significant transaction costs. However, liquidity often dries up at the time when it is most needed. During the Great Financial Crisis in the 2008–2009 period, market liquidity decreased significantly after stock markets suffered steep losses. Bid-ask spreads and price impact increased substantially when market participants demanded liquidity during crisis.

Non-financial risks are difficult to quantify. Measuring direct impact on portfolio value due to regulatory risk, tax risk, accounting risk, legal risk, and other non-financial risks is challenging. However, these non-financial risk factors do contribute to uncertainties embedded in nearly all investments. They should be included in a list of risk factors for the risk management team.

LESSON 6: MANAGING RISK

Candidates should master the following concepts:

- Compute and interpret four risk-adjusted performance measures.

RISK MANAGEMENT

LOS 31j: Demonstrate the use of risk budgeting, position limits, and other methods for managing market risk. Vol 5, pp 181–185

Managing Market Risk

Risk management should have the following characteristics:

1. An effective risk governance model, which allows top management to allocate capital and risk resources effectively across revenue generating divisions.
2. Systems and information technology to provide risk information to top management.
3. Trained personnel to process risk information and make decisions on risk management.

Similar to managing portfolio risk at the individual investor level, to manage risk at the enterprise level, the first objective is to identify the level of risk tolerance. Returns are always associated with risk. There is no return without risk. Given that the amount of risk an enterprise can take is finite, in risk management, we have something called risk budgeting. Risk budgeting allocates risk across divisions in a firm to achieve the optimal overall risk-return tradeoff at the firm level. Note that each division may compete for risk allocations. However, only the top risk management that oversees the firm's overall risk profile may optimally conduct risk budgeting. Risk managers may use the following limits or caps to control risk exposure in a division or an operation:

1. Performance stopouts.
2. Working capital allocations.
3. VAR limits.
4. Scenario analysis limits.
5. Risk factor limits.
6. Position concentration limits.
7. Leverage limits.
8. Liquidity limits.

LOS 31k: Demonstrate the use of exposure limits, marking to market, collateral, netting arrangements, credit standards, and credit derivatives to manage credit risk. Vol 5, pp 185–188

Managing Credit Risk

Credit risk can be managed using some of the following methods:

1. Reduce credit risk by limiting exposure.
2. Reduce credit risk by marking to market.
3. Reduce credit risk by collateral.
4. Reduce credit risk by netting.
5. Reduce credit risk with minimum credit standards and enhanced derivative product companies.
6. Transfer credit risk with credit derivatives.

LOS 31l: Discuss the Sharpe ratio, risk-adjusted return on capital, return over maximum drawdown, and the Sortino ratio as measures of risk-adjusted performance. Vol 5, pp 189–190

Performance Evaluation

Because risk and return are closely associated, it does not make economic sense to evaluate performance based on raw returns without any risk adjustment. Instead, performance measures should have both return and risk dimensions. Performance should be evaluated on a risk adjusted basis. We have the following risk-adjusted return measures.

Sharpe Ratio

The Sharpe ratio is one of the most popular performance measures. It has become the industry standard of risk-adjusted performance benchmark. It measures the reward-to-risk ratio. It measures excess return (over the risk-free rate) per unit of standard deviation of the returns. The higher the Sharpe ratio, the better the performance on a risk-adjusted basis.

$$\text{Sharpe ratio} = \frac{\text{Mean portfolio return} - \text{Risk-free rate}}{\text{Standard deviation of portfolio returns}}$$

Risk-Adjusted Return on Capital (RAROC)

The RAROC general definition is the ratio of expected return on an investment and a measure of the investment's risk. A project or an investment is considered a good one if the RAROC is higher than a certain pre-set benchmark.

Return over Maximum Drawdown (RoMAD)

Maximum drawdown is the maximum difference between a fund's previous high-water mark and its subsequent level. Return over the maximum drawdown is the rate of return of a fund over its drawdown level. If the maximum drawdown is 10 percent and return over it is 18 percent, then the RoMAD ratio is 1.80.

Sortino Ratio

The Sortino ratio measures the excess portfolio return over a minimum acceptable return (MAR) divided by the downside deviation. The Sortino ratio is similar to the Sharpe ratio. The benchmark rate is set to be a MAR instead of the risk-free rate, and the risk measure is set to be downside deviation instead of the standard deviation of the portfolio returns.

$$\text{Sortino ratio} = \frac{\text{Mean portfolio return} - \text{MAR}}{\text{Downside deviation of portfolio returns}}$$

Capital Allocation

An important part of risk management is to directly manage risk. However, capital allocation is a key step in risk management. For example, the size of VAR is proportional to the size of a portfolio. How do you allocate capital across different business divisions of a firm? We have a few strategies listed here.

Nominal, Notional, or Monetary Position Limits

This method sets a maximum amount of capital to be allocated to a business unit. This amount limits the most the business unit is exposed to risk. However, nominal allocation does not necessarily control risk exposure. Two divisions with the same nominal capital allocation may carry significantly different risk exposure.

VAR-Based Position Limits

This method directly addresses risk exposure in a business unit in an enterprise. The advantage of this method is that capital allocation is risk-based, as an allocation should be. However, VAR can be difficult to understand or incorrectly calculated or interpreted. The relation between the enterprise VAR and sum of divisional VARs can also be complicated.

Maximum Loss Limits

The capital allocation is based on the maximum loss limit for each business unit in an enterprise. By using this method, the total amount of risk of the enterprise is no more than the sum of the maximum loss limits over its business units under normal conditions. However, under extreme market conditions, such limits can be reached and exceeded.

Internal Capital Requirements

This method allocates capital based on the management's judgments of what's appropriate for each business unit. The capital ratio (the ratio of capital to assets) or VAR can be used to determine a capital allocation scheme.

Regulatory Capital Requirements

Many financial institutions must satisfy regulatory capital requirements, based on which capital allocations are determined. Note that a capital allocation scheme based on regulatory capital requirements can at times be inconsistent with a rational capital allocation scheme that a firm desires. However, the firm has to conform to the regulatory requirements.

STUDY SESSION 17: RISK MANAGEMENT APPLICATIONS OF DERIVATIVES

READING 32: RISK MANAGEMENT APPLICATIONS OF FORWARD AND FUTURES STRATEGIES

Time to complete: 12 hours

Reading summary: This reading focuses on applications of futures strategies. Specifically, we examine how to use stock index futures, interest rate futures, and currency futures to hedge risks in a portfolio. Stock index futures are used to achieve the following goals: (1) achieve a target beta; (2) construct a synthetic stock index fund using a cash position; (3) construct a synthetic cash position fund using a stock index fund; (4) adjust allocation of a portfolio across equity sectors; and (5) gain exposure to an asset class in advance of committing funds to the asset class. Stock index futures and bond futures are jointly used to adjust the portfolio weights between equity and debt. Currency forward and futures contracts are used to reduce the risk associated with a future receipt or payment in a foreign currency.

LESSON 1: STRATEGIES AND APPLICATIONS FOR MANAGING EQUITY MARKET RISK

RISK MANAGEMENT

Risk management plays an important role both on the investment side and on the corporate side.

On the investment side, modern portfolio theory addresses features of the mean-variance optimal portfolio and states that diversification reduces unsystematic risk of a portfolio. Even if an investor holds a fully diversified portfolio close to the total market index, the investor is still subject to significant market risk, also known as systematic risk, which cannot be diversified away. An effective way to reduce total risk, both systematic and unsystematic, is hedging. Hedging is an important part of risk management and is a commonly used tool by portfolio managers. A risk management team in a financial institution may strategically increase or decrease the exposure of risk factors in their portfolios based on their judgment of future return and risk expectations. Risk management is a crucial part of asset management.

On the corporate side, risk management also plays an important role. Traditional corporate finance theory states that the goal of financial management is to maximize the market value of shareholders' wealth. To achieve this goal, financial managers make optimal investment decisions and financing decisions. Based on the *Discounted Cash Flow* (DCF) approach, the value of the firm's equity is the present value of expected future cash flows accrued to its shareholders. In the DCF analysis, managers prefer higher cash flows (numerator of the DCF) because they generate more wealth to shareholders. Similarly, a smaller discount rate in the DCF analysis results in higher shareholder value. Note that the discount rate reflects the amount of risk in the firm's cash flows. One good way to reduce the discount rate is to reduce the volatility of firm's cash flows. A firm with stable cash flows is perceived to be a firm with low risk. Consequently, investors use a low discount rate to discount the firm's cash flows. Risk management can achieve the goal. By hedging the risk exposures of the firm's balance sheet and operations, a corporate manager can successfully reduce the volatility of the firm's cash flows and make the firm appear less risky to investors.

This reading focuses on how to achieve risk management through the use of futures and forward contracts.

Candidates should master the following hedging and speculation strategies: Increase or decrease an equity portfolio beta by using stock index futures, including neutralize an equity portfolio beta to zero to synthetically create a cash position.

MANAGING EQUITY MARKET RISK

LOS 32a: Demonstrate the use of equity futures contracts to achieve a target beta for a stock portfolio and calculate and interpret the number of futures contracts required. Vol 5, pp 228–232

Managing Equity Risk by Beta Adjustment

Futures are used to manage spot equity positions that are exposed to risk. The risk exposure can be hedged using market index futures, such as the S&P 500 Index futures. Note that market index futures hedges away most of the systematic risk but does not hedge any unsystematic risk. If the goal is to hedge away total risk, including both systematic risk and unsystematic risk, a forward contract that is specifically designed to hedge the underlying unique equity portfolio is an effective instrument. The default risk associated with the forward contract should be considered if a forward contract is used.

Hedging systematic risk is the main concern; beta is used to measure the amount of systematic risk. It is the same beta that is used in the *Capital Asset Pricing Model* (CAPM), where the equity risk is captured in a single factor model based on market returns.

To determine the number of futures contracts required to provide the desired hedge, the following notation is used:

β_S is the current beta of an equity portfolio.

β_T is the target beta of an equity portfolio: the desired level of beta after hedging.

S is the market value of a current equity portfolio.

β_f is the beta of the index futures. It is often close to one, but may not be exactly equal to one.

f is the futures price of market index futures.

N_f is the number of futures contracts needed to hedge the equity portfolio in order to achieve the target beta after hedging is established.

The following relationships based on this notation are:

$$\beta_T S = \beta_S S + N_f \beta_f f$$

$$N_f = \left(\frac{\beta_T - \beta_S}{\beta_f} \right) \left(\frac{S}{f} \right)$$

Example 1-1

An asset management firm holds a diversified stock portfolio with a beta of 1.10. The fund managers are not optimistic about the stock market in the next quarter due to recent upticks in unemployment statistics and volatility in European markets. The managers intend to reduce the risk exposure from a beta of 1.1 to a beta of 0.7 using the S&P 500 Index futures. The market value of the stock portfolio is $12.5 million. The three-month S&P 500 Index futures price is $455,000. The beta of the futures contract is 0.95.

Three months later the overall market decreases by 3.2 percent. The firm's portfolio decreases by 3.5 percent and the S&P 500 Index decreases by 3 percent.

   A. **Compute** the number of futures contracts to be bought or sold to reach the target beta.

   B. **Determine** the total value of the firm's position at the end of three months and calculate the portfolio's effective beta.

Solutions:

   A. This exercise is a very typical CFA Level 3 exam question. Candidates should know it well. The negative sign implies that the firm needs to sell 12 futures contracts.

$$N_f = \left(\frac{\beta_T - \beta_S}{\beta_f} \right)\left(\frac{S}{f} \right) = \left(\frac{0.7 - 1.1}{0.95} \right)\left(\frac{12,500,000}{455,000} \right) = -11.57 \approx -12$$

   B. The portfolio suffered a 3.5 percent loss on $12.5 million. The portfolio value has declined to:

$$12.5 \text{ million} \times (1 - 0.035) = \$12,062,500$$

The futures decreased 3 percent on $455,000. The firm sold futures, so the gain on the sale is:

$$12 \times 455,000 \times 0.03 = \$163,800$$

After considering the hedge, the total value of the portfolio reflects a 2.19 percent loss in value:

$$12,062,500 + 163,800 = \$12,226,300 \qquad \frac{12,226,300}{12,500,000} - 1 = -2.19\%$$

Note that the overall market went down by 3.2 percent. The target beta is 0.70. After hedging, the realized effective beta is 0.6843, which is close to the target beta.

$$\frac{-2.19\%}{-3.2\%} = 0.6843$$

Consider the preceding exercise: a firm may become so bearish that it wishes to totally immunize its risk exposure by reducing its portfolio beta to zero via a futures hedge; the firm will need more futures contracts. The target beta in this case is zero:

$$N_f = \left(\frac{\beta_T - \beta_S}{\beta_f} \right) \left(\frac{S}{f} \right)$$
$$= \left(\frac{0 - 1.1}{0.95} \right) \left(\frac{12,500,000}{455,000} \right)$$
$$= -31.81 \approx -32$$

Selling more futures contracts brings down the portfolio beta further. Using the same realized returns after three months produces the following results:

1. The stock portfolio loses 3.5 percent and declines to: $12,062,500.
2. The futures decreases 3 percent; the short position gains with a hedging profit of: $32 \times 455,000 \times 0.03 = \$436,800$.
3. The total value of the portfolio after taking hedging activities into consideration: $12,062,500 + 436,800 = \$12,499,300$, which reflects a 0.01% loss in value from its initial value of $12.5 million.
4. The overall market loses 3.2 percent, but the hedged portfolio essentially remains unchanged. The realized effective beta is essentially zero, which matches closely with the target beta of zero.

Example 1-2

Super Bull Associates (SBA) is a hedge fund. It currently holds a diversified stock portfolio with a beta of 1.20. Fund managers intend to take an aggressive short-term bet in the market by increasing its portfolio beta to 1.60 over the next two months using S&P 500 Index futures. The market value of the stock portfolio is $80 million. The two-month S&P 500 Index futures contract is priced at $460,000. The beta of the futures contract is 0.97.

After two months the overall market increases by 2.5 percent. SBA's portfolio increases by 3.2 percent and the S&P 500 Index increases by 2.4 percent.

A. **Compute** the number of futures contracts to be bought or sold to reach the target beta.

B. **Determine** the total value of the firm's position at the end of two months and calculate the portfolio's effective beta.

Solutions:

A. Solve for the number of contracts:

$$N_f = \left(\frac{\beta_T - \beta_S}{\beta_f}\right)\left(\frac{S}{f}\right)$$

$$= \left(\frac{1.6 - 1.2}{0.97}\right)\left(\frac{80,000,000}{460,000}\right)$$

$$= 71.72 \approx 72$$

The managers need to buy 72 S&P 500 Index futures to increase the beta of the portfolio from 1.20 to 1.60.

B. The portfolio gained 3.2 percent on $80 million; the value has increased to:

$$80 \text{ million} \times (1 + 0.032) = \$82.56 \text{ million}$$

The futures increased 2.4 percent on $460,000. The firm bought futures, so the gain equals:

$$72 \times 460,000 \times 0.024 = \$794,880$$

The overall position, after hedging activities, reflects a 4.19 percent gain in value:

$$82,560,000 + 794,880 = \$83,354,880$$

$$\frac{83,354,880}{80,000,000} - 1 = 4.19\%$$

Note that the overall market went up by 2.5 percent. The target beta is 1.60. After hedging, the realized effective beta is 1.6774, which is close to the target beta.

$$\frac{4.19\%}{2.5\%} = 1.6774$$

LOS 32b: Construct a synthetic stock index fund using cash and stock index futures (equitizing cash). Vol 5, pp 233–236

LOS 32c: Explain the use of stock index futures to convert a long stock position into synthetic cash. Vol 5, pp 237–241

Creating Synthetic Equity or Cash Positions

The beta of an equity portfolio can be decreased to zero by selling an appropriate number of stock index futures. As expressed in equation 1, when the portfolio beta is zero, the portfolio of long stock and short futures can be viewed as a risk-free bond (ignoring unsystematic risk). Equation 1 turns around to produce equation 2, which demonstrates that buying the risk-free bond and the futures can replicate a position in the stock.

> (1) Long stock + Short futures = Long risk-free bond
> (2) Long stock = Long risk-free bond + Long futures

Additional notation is needed to determine the number of futures contracts required so that the portfolio of the long futures position and a risk-free bond exactly replicates the underlying stock index:

V is the amount of money to be invested.

f is the futures price of market index futures.

q is the price multiplier of the futures contract (e.g., for the S&P Index futures, it is $250).

T is the time to maturity of the futures contract.

r is the risk-free interest rate.

δ is the dividend yield of the market index.

S_t is the level of stock index at time t.

N_f is the number of futures contracts.

N_f^* is the rounded (whole number) number of futures contracts.

> (2) Long stock = Long risk-free bond + Long futures

The goal is to create a synthetic stock position, the equivalent of owning the stock and reinvesting the dividends. The futures price at expiration converges to the spot price at T. The futures payoff is the difference between the amount received at expiration and the amount paid for the futures contracts; it can be expressed as:

> (3) Futures payoff = $N_f^* q \, (S_T - f)$ or
>
> (4) Futures payoff = $(N_f^* q S_T) - (N_f^* q f)$

Money is invested, today, in bonds at the risk-free rate to accumulate to the second term in equation 4, the amount to settle the futures contract. The amount invested is the present value of that term and given there is V amount of capital today to invest, the relationship is expressed as:

$$V = \frac{(N_f^* q f)}{(1+r)^T}$$

The preceding formula can be used to solve for N_f^*, the number of futures contracts (rounded to the nearest integer):

$$N_f^* = \frac{V(1+r)^T}{fq}$$

Note the actual amount of capital invested today is not V but V^*, because it will be based on the rounded number of futures contracts N_f^*.

The number of units of stock equivalent to investing V^* and purchasing N_f^* futures contracts can be expressed as:

$$\text{Unit of stock} = N_f q \frac{1}{(1+\delta)^T}$$

Similar to futures contracts, only whole numbers of shares of stock index are bought; the above expression is rounded to the nearest integer.

To summarize, in this synthetic transaction, it's as if the investor began with $N_f q (1/(1+\delta)^T)$ units of stock and collected and reinvested dividends. The stock is never owned. The investor synthetically ends up with the equivalent of $N_f q$ units of stock at expiration.

Example 1-3

A fund manager creates a synthetic index fund that tracks the S&P 500 Index with a portfolio value of $50 million. The manager plans to hold the position for the next three months. The three-month S&P 500 Index futures contract is priced at $1,840 with a price multiplier of $250. Dividend yield on the S&P 500 Index is estimated to be 1.8 percent and the three-month risk-free rate is 4 percent.

    A.   **Determine** the number of S&P 500 Index futures the manager buys/sells to create the synthetic position and **calculate** the number of shares involved in the transaction.

    B.   **Analyze** the outcome at the end of three months.

Solutions:

    A.   The number of futures contracts and the number of shares is:

$$N_f^* = \frac{V(1+r)^T}{fq}$$

$$= \left(\frac{50 \text{ million} \times (1.04)^{3/12}}{1,840 \times 250} \right)$$

$$= 109.77 \approx 110$$

$$\text{Number of shares} = N_f^* q = \frac{1}{(1+\delta)^T}$$

$$= 110 \times 250 \frac{1}{(1.018)^{3/12}}$$

$$= 27,377.62 \approx 27,378$$

B. The portfolio manager needs to buy 110 S&P 500 Index futures to create a synthetic index fund. Because of rounding, the amount synthetically invested in stock is:

$$V^* = \frac{N_f^* \times qf}{(1+r)^T}$$

$$= \frac{110 \times 250 \times 1{,}840}{(1.04)^{3/12}}$$

$$= \$50{,}106{,}282$$

The above amount is slightly more than $50 million because we round up N_f to N_f. The portfolio manager invests this amount in risk-free bonds; in three months this amount will grow to:

$$\$50{,}106{,}282 \times 1.04^{3/12} = \$50{,}600{,}000$$

The number of shares at the beginning of the hedge is 27,377.62. Due to reinvestment of dividend income, at the end of the hedging period the number of shares would have grown to:

$$27{,}377.62 \times 1.018^{3/12} = 27{,}500$$

The futures contract payoff is:

$$N_f^* q = (S_T - f)$$

$$= 110(250)(S_T - 1{,}840)$$

$$= 27{,}500 S_T - \$50.6 \text{ million}$$

The portfolio manager would pay $50.6 million to settle the futures contract. Note that the above amount $50.6 million is exactly the future value (at the risk-free rate of 4 percent) of $50,106,282.

The portfolio manager has synthetically created his equity portfolio; upon settling the futures contract, he effectively has 27,500 units of the index.

Just as a synthetic equity position can be created, so too can a synthetic cash position be created. Instead of purchasing futures contracts, the portfolio manager will sell futures contracts. The equations are as follows:

$$N_f^* = \frac{V(1+r)^T}{fq}$$

$$V^* = \frac{-N_f^* qf}{(1+r)^T}$$

Stock in the amount of V^* has been synthetically converted to cash. Similarly, because dividends are assumed to be reinvested, the number of units of stock at the start and at expiration is calculated the same; they are just assumed to be sold.

Example 1-4

Synthetic Trading Solutions (STS) is an equity trading firm that uses derivative contracts in its risk management. Mika Jones, CFA, an STS portfolio manager, holds a $40 million stock portfolio that tracks the performance of the Dow Jones Industrial Average (DJIA) Index. The DJIA Index has a dividend yield of 2.8 percent. Jones is extremely concerned about the performance of the DJIA Index over the next three months and believes she should be out of the market during this period of time. She uses DJIA Index futures to convert the portfolio position to a cash position. The current three-month DJIA Index futures contract is priced at $16,100 with a price multiplier of $100. The risk-free rate is 5 percent per year.

    A.   **Calculate** the number of DJIA Index futures contracts Jones should buy/sell.

    B.   **Calculate** the dollar amount of stock synthetically converted to cash.

    C.   **Calculate** the number of DJIA Index shares involved in the transaction.

    D.   **Analyze** the outcome at expiration of the futures contract.

Solutions:

    A.   Jones is creating a synthetic cash position. The number of futures contracts to be sold, rounded to the nearest integer, is:

$$N_f^* = \frac{V(1+r)^T}{fq}$$

$$= \left(\frac{40 \text{ million} \times (1.05)^{3/12}}{16,100 \times 100} \right)$$

$$= -25.15 \approx -25$$

    B.   Based on this number of futures contracts, the dollar amount of stock synthetically converted to cash is:

$$V^* = \frac{-N_f^* \times qf}{(1+r)T}$$

$$= \frac{25 \times 250 \times 16,100}{(1.05)^{3/12}}$$

$$= \$39,762,031$$

    C.   The number of shares rounded to the nearest integer:

$$\text{Rounded number of shares} = N_f^* q = \frac{1}{(1+\delta)T}$$

$$= 25 \times 100 \frac{1}{(1.028)^{3/12}}$$

$$= 2,482.8 \approx 2,483$$

D. The portfolio manager needs to sell 25 DJIA Index futures to bring the stock portfolio to a cash position. Because of rounding, the amount of stock value ($39,762,031) that it is synthetically converted to is slightly lower than $40 million because N_f rounds down to N_f^*.

The number of shares is 2482.8 shares at the beginning of the hedge. Due to reinvestment of dividend income, the number of shares grows at the rate of $\delta = 2.8\%$ to $2{,}482.8 \times 1.028^{3/12} = 2{,}500$ shares at the end of the hedging period. The position includes:

- Futures contract payoff:

$$N_f^* q = (S_T - f)$$
$$= -25(100)(S_T - 16{,}100)$$
$$= -25{,}00 S_T - \$40.25 \text{ million}$$

- Stock equal to: $+ 2{,}500 S_T$

The positions above net to a value of $40.25 million, which is exactly the future value (at the risk-free rate of 5 percent) of $39,762,031.

LESSON 2: ASSET ALLOCATION WITH FUTURES

Candidates should master the following hedging and speculation strategies: Use stock index futures and bond futures to change the asset allocation weights in a stock and bond portfolio from an existing allocation to a target allocation.

LOS 32d: Demonstrate the use of equity and bond futures to adjust the allocation of a portfolio between equity and debt. Vol 5, pp 241–248

Adjusting Asset Allocation with Futures Contracts

Asset allocation contributes more to superior performance than to security selection and superior performance depends on maintaining optimal asset allocation over time. Changes in asset allocation generally incur trading costs, such as brokerage fees and commissions, bid-ask spreads, and pricing impact, among others. Frequent asset allocation changes tend to be cost prohibitive.

Financial derivative contracts can be used efficiently to temporarily alter a portfolio's asset allocation. The following example demonstrates how to reallocate a portfolio using stock index futures and bond futures.

Market Timer Group is an asset management firm that specializes in strategically rotating its investments among stocks, bonds, and cash. Currently, the fund's *assets under management* (AUM) of $200 million are allocated 70 percent in stocks and 30 percent in bonds. The stock portion of the portfolio has a beta of 1.20 and the bond portion of the portfolio has a duration of 12. Fund managers intend to avoid an expected three-month market correction by reallocating to 40 percent stocks and 60 percent bonds using futures contracts. The stock index futures contract carries a futures price of $355,000 and a beta of 0.98. The bond futures contract carries a futures price of $124,500 and a modified duration of 9.6. Analyze the mangers' action to achieve their target allocation weights.

To reduce stock exposure without liquidating the stock portfolio, the managers sell stock index futures, synthetically creating a cash position and reducing the existing stock position. (This could also be accomplished by synthetically reducing portfolio beta, but that is not applicable to this case.) The managers can then use the synthetic cash to increase the bond allocation by purchasing bond futures.

Here is how the strategy is implemented:

1. Original stock value: $200 \times 0.70 = \$140$ million. Original bond value: $200 \times 0.30 = \$60$ million.
2. Target stock value: $200 \times 0.40 = \$80$ million. Target bond value: $200 \times 0.60 = \$120$ million.
3. The firm "synthetically" sells $60 million of stocks and "synthetically" buys $60 million of bonds to reach its goal.
4. On the stock side, the number of stock index futures (N_{sf}) the firm needs to sell equals 207. β_T, β_S, β_T represents the target beta, stock beta, and futures beta, respectively. S, f_S is the market value of the stock to be "sold" and the stock index futures price, respectively.

$$N_{sf} = \left(\frac{\beta_T - \beta_S}{\beta_f} \right) \left(\frac{S}{f_s} \right)$$
$$= \left(\frac{0 - 1.20}{0.98} \right) \left(\frac{60,000,000}{355,000} \right)$$
$$= -206.95 \approx -207$$

5. The firm needs to buy 602 bond futures, N, $MDUR_T$, $MDUR_B$, $MDUR_f$ is target modified duration, modified duration of the existing bonds (the cash position), and implied modified duration of the futures, respectively. B, f_B is the market value of the bonds and the bonds futures price, respectively.

$$N_{sf} = \left(\frac{MDUR_T - MDUR_B}{MDUR_f} \right) \left(\frac{B}{f_B} \right)$$
$$= \left(\frac{12 - 0}{9.6} \right) \left(\frac{60,000,000}{124,500} \right)$$
$$= 602.41 \approx 602$$

In summary, the firm should sell 207 stock index futures and buy 602 bond futures to change the portfolio's asset allocation to its desired allocation of 40 percent in stocks and 60 percent in bonds. The stock index futures and bond futures have three months to maturity, which matches the time horizon over which the firm intends to alter the asset allocation.

Three months later, the stock portfolio realizes a return of –5 percent and the bond portfolio realizes a return of 3 percent. The stock index futures price decreases from $355,000 to $338,000 and the bond futures price increases from $124,500 to $127,700.

Dollar gains and losses of futures positions and value of spot positions are given below:

1. Gains on stock index futures: $207 \times (355,000 - 338,000) = \$3,519.000$
2. Gains on bond futures: $602 \times (127,700 - 124,500) = \$1,926,400$
3. Value of stock portion of portfolio: $140,000,000 \times (1 - 0.05) = \$133,000,000$
4. Value of bond portion of portfolio: $60,000,000 \times (1 + 0.03) = \$61,800,000$
5. Total value of the portfolio with futures transactions: sum of #1 through #4 = $200,245,400$

The value of a portfolio with the target 40 percent of stocks and 60 percent of bonds is: $200,000,000 \times 0.4 \times (1 - 0.05) + 200,000,000 \times 0.6 \times (1 + 0.03) = \$199,600,000$. The value of the synthetically created portfolio is slightly higher than that of the target portfolio by $200,245,400/199,600,000 - 1 = 0.32$ percent.

LOS 32e: Demonstrate the use of futures to adjust the allocation of a portfolio across equity sectors and to gain exposure to an asset class in advance of actually committing funds to the asset class. Vol 5, pp 248–250

Example 2-1

A private wealth management firm services a high net worth client who holds a $50 million portfolio of technology stocks. The portfolio has a beta of 1.20. Over the next two months, the client instructs the fund managers to temporarily exchange $10 million of the existing portfolio to $10 million of a total market ETF, which has a beta of 1.02. The fund managers intend to use stock index futures to synthetically change the allocation over the next two months. They identified that the NASDAQ 100 Index futures and the S&P 500 Index futures are best for this purpose. The NASDAQ 100 Index futures contract has a beta of 1.15, a two-month futures price of $4,010, and a price multiplier of $100. The S&P 500 Index futures contract has a beta of 0.96, a two-month futures price of $1,810, and a price multiplier of $250.

At the end of the two months, all sectors of the market suffer negative returns. The client's tech-stock portfolio loses 4.6 percent. The NASDAQ 100 Index futures contract loses 4.7 percent. The total market ETF loses 4 percent. The S&P 500 Index futures contract loses 3.9 percent.

A. **Determine** the appropriate trades to achieve the client's goal.

B. **Analyze** the client's portfolio value at the end of two months.

Solutions:

A. Two transactions are required.

First, to synthetically reduce the existing holding of technology stocks by $10 million, the managers sell X number of NASDAQ 100 Index futures. This effectively converts the $10 million into cash and converts the beta to zero. Second, the managers synthetically purchase $10 million of total market ETF. To achieve the second goal, they buy Y number of S&P 500 Index futures. The beta now converts from zero to 1.02, the beta of the desired total market ETF.

$$X = \left(\frac{\beta_T - \beta_S}{\beta_{fNASDAQ}} \right)\left(\frac{S}{f_{NASDAQ}} \right) = \left(\frac{0 - 1.20}{1.15} \right)\left(\frac{10,000,000}{4,010 \times 100} \right) = -26.02 \approx -26$$

$$Y = \left(\frac{\beta_{ETF} - \beta_T}{\beta_{S\&P}} \right)\left(\frac{S}{f_{S\&P}} \right) = \left(\frac{1.02 - 0}{0.96} \right)\left(\frac{10,000,000}{1,810 \times 250} \right) = 23.48 \approx 23$$

Managers should sell 26 NASDAQ 100 Index futures and buy 23 S&P 500 Index futures to synthetically create the desired allocation.

B. The target portfolio allocation is $40 million in existing tech stocks and $10 million in the total market ETF. The ending value of the portfolio with the target allocation is:

$$[40 \times (1 - 0.046)] + [10 \times (1 - 0.04)] = \$47.76 \text{ million}$$

The synthetically constructed portfolio has three components: $50 million of the original tech-stocks, a short position in the NASDAQ 100 Index futures, and a long position in the S&P 500 Index futures. The ending value of the synthetic portfolio is:

$$[50 \text{ million} \times (1 - 0.046)] + [(-26 \times 4,010 \times 100 \times -0.047)] + [(23 \times 1,810 \times 250 \times -0.039)] = \$47.78 \text{ million}$$

Conclusions: The value of the synthetically constructed position is only 0.05 percent different from that of the target position; therefore, the synthetic strategy works effectively.

The following application exercise demonstrates how to adjust allocation weights between one bond class and another.

Example 2-2

A bond fund strategically changes its allocations in long-term and short-term bonds by predictions of long-term and short-term interest rate movements based on economic indicators. Currently, the fund holds a bond portfolio with a market value of $100 million and a modified duration of 12.4. Over the next three months, managers of the fund intend to hold $20 million of cash equivalents and increase the modified duration of the remaining bond portfolio from 12.4 to 13.9. Fund managers plan to use bond futures to achieve this change in allocation. Bond futures contracts have a futures price of $133,500 and a modified duration of 7.59. For the purposes of their analysis, the managers use a modified duration for cash equivalents of 0.25.

At the end of the three months, interest rates increase by 1.2 percent across all maturities. Bond futures price decreases from $133,500 to $119,800.

A.   **Determine** the appropriate trades to achieve the goal.

B.   **Analyze** the bond portfolio performance at the end of three months.

Solutions:

A.   The target bond portfolio should carry a modified duration:

$$\frac{20}{100} \times 0.25 + \frac{80}{100} \times 13.9 = 11.17$$

$$N_f = \left(\frac{MDUR_T - MDUR_B}{MDUR_f} \right)\left(\frac{B}{f} \right)$$

$$= \left(\frac{11.17 - 12.4}{7.59} \right)\left(\frac{100,000,000}{133,500} \right)$$

$$= -121.39 \approx -121$$

The duration needs to change from 12.4 to 11.17 on the entire portfolio size of $100 million and not $20 million. Alternatively, the same result is reached by reducing duration from 12.4 to 0.25 on $20 million and increasing duration from 12.4 to 13.9 on $80 million. The sum of two numbers of bond futures is the same as 121 above.

$$N_f = \left(\frac{MDUR_T - MDUR_B}{MDUR_f} \right)\left(\frac{B}{f} \right)$$

$$= \left(\frac{0.25 - 12.4}{7.59} \right)\left(\frac{20,000,000}{133,500} \right)$$

$$= -239.82$$

$$N_f = \left(\frac{MDUR_T - MDUR_B}{MDUR_f} \right) \left(\frac{B}{f} \right)$$

$$= \left(\frac{13.9 - 12.4}{7.59} \right) \left(\frac{80,000,000}{133,500} \right)$$

$$= 118.43$$

$$-239.82 + 118.43 = -121.39$$

Managers should sell 121 bond futures to synthetically create the desired allocation.

B.   At the end of three months, interest rates increase by 1.2 percent and all bond values decrease. The size of the decrease is determined by the product of interest rate change and bond modified duration. The value of the bond portfolio with the target allocation is:

$$100 \text{ million} \times (1 - 0.012 \times 11.17) = \$86.596 \text{ million}$$

The synthetically constructed portfolio has two components: $100 million of the original bond portfolio with a modified duration of 12.4, a short position in 121 bond futures. The value of the synthetic portfolio is:

$$[100 \text{ million} \times (1 - 0.012 \times 12.4)] + [-121 \times (119,800 - 133,500)]$$
$$= \$86.778 \text{ million}$$

Conclusions: The value of the synthetically constructed position is only 0.21 percent different from that of the target position; therefore, the synthetic strategy works effectively.

The following application exercise demonstrates how to adjust allocation weights between bonds and stocks.

Example 2-3

Alpha Traders Inc. is an active trading firm that frequently changes its asset allocations based on short-term predictions of stock market and bond market returns. The firm currently holds a $100 million portfolio; 60 percent of the assets are allocated to stocks and the remaining 40 percent are in bonds. The stock portfolio has a beta of 1.05 and the bond portfolio has a modified duration of 8.8. The firm predicts (1) a significant positive return in the stock market over the next month and (2) an increase in bond yield over the next month. Consequently, the firm intends to change its asset allocation to 75 percent in stocks and 25 percent in bonds. Additionally, the firm intends to increase its stock portfolio beta from 1.05 to 1.25 and to decrease its bond portfolio duration from 8.8 to 6.8. Stock market index futures contracts are priced at $466,000 with a beta of 0.97. Bond futures contracts are priced at $128,600 with a modified duration of 6.89.

At the end of the month, the stock portfolio increases by 5.2 percent and the stock index futures price increases to $488,200. During the month, interest rates increase by 0.8 percent across all maturities. Bond futures price decreases to $121,500.

    A.   **Determine** the appropriate trades to achieve a desired synthetic position.

    B.   **Analyze** the portfolio performance at the end of the month.

Solutions:

    A.   On the bond side, there are two trades: (1) synthetically sell $15 million of bonds to reduce the asset allocation weight on bond portfolio to the desired 25 percent, and (2) synthetically reduce the bond modified duration from 8.8 to 6.8 on $25 million remaining bonds.

$$N_{f1Bonds} = \left(\frac{MDUR_T - MDUR_B}{MDUR_f} \right)\left(\frac{B}{f} \right)$$

$$= \left(\frac{0 - 8.8}{6.89} \right)\left(\frac{15,000,000}{128,600} \right)$$

$$= -148.98 \approx -149$$

$$N_{f2Bonds} = \left(\frac{MDUR_T - MDUR_B}{MDUR_f} \right)\left(\frac{B}{f} \right)$$

$$= \left(\frac{6.8 - 8.8}{6.89} \right)\left(\frac{25,000,000}{128,600} \right)$$

$$= -56.429 \approx -56$$

$$-149 + (-56) = -205$$

On the stock side, there are two trades: (1) synthetically buy $15 million of stocks to increase the asset allocation weight on stocks to the desired 75 percent, (2) synthetically increase the beta from 1.05 to 1.25 on a $75 million of stock portfolio.

$$N_{f1Stock} = \left(\frac{\beta_T - \beta_S}{\beta_f} \right)\left(\frac{S}{f} \right)$$

$$= \left(\frac{1.05 - 0}{0.97} \right)\left(\frac{15,000,000}{466,000} \right)$$

$$= 34.84 \approx 35$$

$$N_{f2Stock} = \left(\frac{\beta_T - \beta_S}{\beta_f} \right)\left(\frac{S}{f} \right)$$

$$= \left(\frac{1.25 - 1.05}{0.97} \right)\left(\frac{75,000,000}{466,000} \right)$$

$$= 33.18 \approx 33$$

$$35 + 33 = 68$$

Managers should sell 205 bond futures and buy 68 stock index futures to synthetically create the desired allocation.

B. On the bond side, the target position is $25 million bonds with a duration of 6.8. After a 0.8 percent yield curve shift, the value of the target bond position is:

$$\$25 \text{ million} \times [1 - (0.008 \times 6.8)] = \$23.64 \text{ million}$$

The synthetically constructed bond position has two components: $40 million of the original bond with a modified duration of 8.8, a short position in 205 bond futures. The bond position has lost value, but the short position has gained. The ending value of the synthetic portfolio is:

$$\$40 \text{ million} \times [1 - 0.008 \times 8.8] + [-205 \times (121,500 - 128,600)]$$
$$= \$38.64 \text{ million}$$

On the stock side, the target position is $75 million stocks. The value of the target stock position is:

$$\$75 \text{ million} \times (1 + 0.052) = \$78.90 \text{ million}$$

The synthetically constructed stock position has two components: $60 million of the original stocks with a beta of 1.05 and a long position in 68 stock index futures. The ending value of the synthetic portfolio is:

$$\$60 \text{ million} \times (1 + 0.052) + 68 \times (488,200 - 466,000) = \$64.63 \text{ million}$$

Putting the stock and bond positions together results in:

Target portfolio value = 23.64 + 78.90 = $102.54 million

Synthetic portfolio value = 38.64 + 64.63 = $103.27 million

Conclusions: The value of the synthetically constructed position is 0.7 percent different from that of the target position; therefore, the synthetic strategy works effectively.

Stock index futures and bond futures may also be used to take immediate synthetic market positions before funding becomes available to invest in the underlying spot market. They allow an investor to be in the market when investment opportunities are attractive when funding for investments is not yet available.

Example 2-4

Alpha Traders Inc. is an active trading firm that frequently changes its asset allocations based on short-term predictions of stock market and bond market returns. An existing client informs the firm that there will be $10 million available for investment in three months. Fund managers in this firm have predicted strongly positive returns in both the stock market and the bond market for the next three months starting today. The client would like to participate in the market performance even though funding won't be available for the next three months. Fund managers state that they can use futures contracts to achieve this goal. The client's asset allocation is 70 percent in stocks with a beta of 1.10 and 30 percent in bonds with a modified duration of 7.8. Stock index futures contracts are priced at $375,000 with a beta of 0.97. Bond futures contracts are priced at $116,800 with a modified duration of 6.9.

At the end of the three months, the target stock portfolio increases 4.7 percent and the bond portfolio increases 2.4 percent. The stock index futures contract price increases to $391,200. The bond futures contract price increases to $119,400.

A. **Determine** the appropriate trades to achieve a desired synthetic position.

B. **Analyze** the portfolio performance after three months.

Solutions:

A. The synthetic position would involve long stock index futures and long bond futures.

$$N_{fBonds} = \left(\frac{MDUR_T - MDUR_B}{MDUR_f} \right)\left(\frac{B}{f} \right)$$

$$= \left(\frac{7.80 - 0}{6.90} \right)\left(\frac{3,000,000}{116,800} \right)$$

$$= 29.04 \approx 29$$

$$N_{fStock} = \left(\frac{\beta_T - \beta_S}{\beta_f} \right)\left(\frac{S}{f} \right)$$

$$= \left(\frac{1.10 - 0}{0.97} \right)\left(\frac{7,000,000}{375,000} \right)$$

$$= 21.17 \approx 21$$

The fund manager should buy 29 bond futures and 21 stock index futures today to synthetically construct a portfolio to replicate the target position.

B. Gains from the stock index futures and bond futures:

$$21 \times (391,200 - 375,000) = \$340,200$$

$$29 \times (119,400 - 116,800) = \$75,400$$

$$340,200 + 75,400 = \$415,600$$

Gains from target stock and bond portfolio:

$$7 \text{ million} \times (0.047) + 3 \text{ million} \times (0.024) = \$401,000$$

Note that by using stock index futures and bond futures the firm generates a speculative gain of \$415,600, which mimics the gain of \$401,000 in the target portfolio of stocks and bonds.

LESSON 3: STRATEGIES AND APPLICATIONS FOR MANAGING FOREIGN CURRENCY RISK

Candidates should master the following hedging and speculation strategies: Use currency forward and/or futures contracts to change currency risk exposure of an expected spot position

LOS 32f: Explain exchange rate risk and demonstrate the use of forward contracts to reduce the risk associated with a future receipt or payment in a foreign currency. Vol 5, pp 250–254

MANAGING FOREIGN CURRENCY RISK

As the global financial markets and product markets integrate, firms' operations as well as their balance sheets are increasingly exposed to cash flows denominated in foreign currencies. Consequently, firms' bottom lines are subject to price volatility in the foreign currency market. Hedging currency risk becomes an important part of corporate risk management. Proper risk control in foreign currency reduces volatility of firms' earnings and cash flows, reduces corporate risks perceived by investors, reduces cost of capital of the firm, and eventually enhances firm value.

The following application exercises demonstrate how to use forward and futures contracts to hedge a firm's committed cash inflows and cash outflows denominated in a foreign currency.

Example 3-1

Zippy Airlines is a startup airline and intends to build its fleet of new aircrafts by purchasing €400 million of Airbus planes. The purchase contract is signed at the beginning of the year and the transaction will take place at the end of the year.

Zippy is a U.S. firm and all its financial statements are prepared in U.S. dollars. Risk managers at Zippy are concerned about foreign currency risk embedded in the purchase contract. If the euro appreciates against the U.S. dollar significantly between now and the end of the year, the firm will have to pay significantly more in U.S. dollars to buy the fleet of planes. The risk manager considers using a currency forward contract to hedge. Currently, in December, the forward contract price is $1.36/€.

At the end of the year, the spot euro price is $1.23/€.

A. **Determine** the appropriate hedge at the start of the year.

B. **Discuss** the firm's actions and cash flows at the end of the year.

Solutions:

A. Given the firm needs to buy euro in the future to satisfy the purchase contract, to hedge, the firm should buy euro forward. The risk manager should buy €400 million forward at the current forward price of $1.36/€. Note that there is no cash flow today at the signing of the forward agreement, and that the buyer (the firm) and seller (maybe a forward dealer) are both exposed to the credit (default) risk of the other party.

B. The firm takes delivery of €400 million from the forward dealer and the firm pays 400 × 1.36 = $544 million of U.S. dollars to the forward dealer. The firm applies the €400 million to the purchase contract. The firm locks in a fixed euro price of $1.36/€ at the beginning of the year when the purchase contract was signed.

Example 3-2

Hollywood Inc. is an independent U.S. movie production company. The company signs a contract at the beginning of the year on five action movies with a Chinese media distributor. The five movies will be released in China this summer. The contract is quoted in the Chinese currency (RMB) in the amount of 1 billion RMB. Payment will be made on June 1, right before the movies are released in China.

Hollywood Inc. is concerned about foreign currency risk embedded in the contract. If the RMB depreciates against the U.S. dollar significantly between now and June, the firm will suffer financial losses. The firm's consultants suggest using currency forward contracts to hedge against currency fluctuations. Currently, June forward price of RMB is $0.16/RMB.

On June 1, spot RMB price turns out to be $0.14/RMB.

A. **Determine** the appropriate hedge.

B. **Discuss** the firm's actions and cash flows on June 1.

> **Solutions:**
>
> A. The U.S. firm will receive foreign currency (RMB) in June that it intends to exchange for USD in June. The firm should sell RMB forward. The firm should sell 1 billion RMB forward at the current June forward price of $0.16/RMB. By signing this forward contract, the firm agrees to deliver 1 billion RMB in June in exchange for $160 million. The firm locks in a dollar value of the 1 billion RMB today.
>
> B. The firm collects 1 billion RMB from the movie sales contract and delivers the 1 billion RMB to the buyer of the forward contract. The buyer of the forward contract makes a payment of $160 million to the firm. The spot RMB price of $0.14/RMB does not play a role in the transaction because the transaction is completed in the forward market, not the spot market. If the firm did not construct the hedge, the firm would be forced to sell RMB at $0.14/RMB, which is a less attractive ex-post price.

LOS 32g: Explain the limitations to hedging the exchange rate risk of a foreign market portfolio and discuss feasible strategies for managing such risk. Vol 5, pp 254–258

In the above exercises, the sizes of the cash flows are known with certainty because the sizes of cash flows are already clearly stated in the purchase or sales contracts. In reality, in the context of asset management, the sizes of cash flows are generally unknown. For example, on July 1, a portfolio manager who controls €20 million of foreign stocks would like to hedge the terminal value of the portfolio at the end of the year. Note that the value of the portfolio is subject to two risk factors: (1) the performance of the stock portfolio measured in the local currency, €, and (2) the exchange rate between euro and U.S. dollar. The manager can use stock index futures contracts to at least partially hedge the first risk factor and can use foreign currency forward contracts to hedge the second risk factor. Note that with the stock index futures alone, the stock portfolio is synthetically transformed into a foreign risk-free bond. Now, adding currency forward, the foreign risk-free bond is subsequently synthetically transformed into a domestic risk-free bond. Portfolio managers do not want to perform the above two hedging transactions all the time because they need to stay in the stock market to generate returns (and fees). The above hedging strategies are useful only for short term to avoid perceived temporary market downside risks.

> **Example 3-3**
>
> A U.S. portfolio manager who controls €20 million of foreign stocks is concerned about the downside risk in the euro zone stock market in the next three months. The manager prefers to lock in a terminal value denominated in U.S. dollars at the end of the third month, so that the portfolio is free of equity market risk as well as foreign currency risk.
>
> The market value of the stock portfolio is €20 million and the beta of the portfolio is 1.15. A three-month stock index futures contract in the euro zone is priced at €275,200 with a beta of 0.95. The three-month euro zone risk-free rate is 4 percent on a money market yield basis. The three-month U.S. risk-free rate is 3 percent on a money market yield basis. The spot exchange rate is $1.3000/€. The manager would use a dollar-denominated forward contract on the euro to hedge currency risk; the contract is priced at $1.2968/€.

Three months later, the stock portfolio loses 4.2 percent of its value. The euro zone stock index futures contract price decreases to €263,350. Spot euro price becomes $1.33/€.

    A.   **Construct** a hedging strategy so that the portfolio is free of both equity risk and currency risk.

    B.   **Compute** the manager's cash flows at the end of three months.

Solutions:

    A.   To hedge equity risk, the firm sells foreign stock index futures. The number of stock index futures is:

$$N_f = \left(\frac{\beta_T - \beta_S}{\beta_f} \right)\left(\frac{S}{f} \right)$$

$$= \left(\frac{0 - 1.15}{0.95} \right)\left(\frac{20,000,000}{275,200} \right)$$

$$= -87.97 \approx -88$$

The stock portfolio and a short position in 88 stock index futures approximately (due to rounding, cross hedge, and basis risk) synthetically replicates a long foreign risk-free bond position, which expects to yield a return of 4 percent in the euro zone. The target future value at the end of the third month in euros is:

$$€20,000,000 \times \left(1 + 0.04 \times \frac{90}{360} \right) = €20,200,000$$

The portfolio manager enters a currency forward contract to sell €20,200,000 forward at $1.2968/€ and locks in a U.S. dollar value of the target terminal value, which in U.S. dollars is:

$$€20.2 \text{ million} \times 1.2968 = \$26.1954 \text{ million}$$

Note that the above value is close to (subject to rounding errors) the terminal value of a three-month U.S. risk-free bond, if the foreign stock portfolio is liquidated and converted to U.S. dollars to buy a risk-free bond today:

$$€20 \text{ million} \times 1.3000 \times \left(1 + 0.03 \, \frac{90}{360} \right) = \$26.1950 \text{ million}$$

To hedge both equity risk in the euro zone and the currency risk in euros, the portfolio manager needs to sell 88 foreign stock index futures and enter into a forward contract with the notional principal of €20,200,000 priced at $1.2968/€.

    B.   The initial value of the portfolio in U.S. dollars is:

$$\$26 \text{ million (€2.0 million at } \$1.3/€)$$

At the end of three months, the stock portfolio value loses 4.2 percent:

$$€20 \text{ million} \times (1 - 0.042) = €19.16 \text{ million}$$

If the manager does not hedge at all, there is a loss of 1.9% and the terminal value in U.S. dollars is:

$$€19.16 \text{ million} \times 1.33 = \$25.4828 \text{ million}$$

$$\frac{25.4828}{26.0000} - 1 = -0.0199 = 1.9\% \text{ loss}$$

The position of short 88 stock index futures generates a hedging gain of:

$$-88 \times (263,350 - 275,200) = €1,042,800$$

The combined sum of the stock portfolio and the gain on the short index futures is €20,202,800. This amount is a gain of 1.01%, which, as expected, approximates the euro zone (foreign) risk-free rate (annualized return of 4%):

$$\frac{€20,202,800}{€20,000,000} - 1 = 0.01014 = 1.01\% \text{ gain}$$

If the manager hedges only equity risk using stock index futures, and does not hedge currency risk, when converted to U.S. dollars, there is a gain of 3.3% and the terminal value in U.S. dollars is:

$$€20,202,800 \times 1.33 = \$26.8697 \text{ million}$$

$$\frac{26.8697}{26.0000} - 1 = 0.03345 = 3.3\% \text{ gain}$$

The manager sold €20,200,000 in the forward market at \$1.2968/€. The spot price is \$1.33/€. The contract settles at a loss:

$$-€20,200,000 \times (1.33 - 1.2968) = -\$670,640$$

If the manager hedges both the equity risk and the currency risk, when converted to U.S. dollars, the gain is 0.77%, which, as expected, approximates the U.S. (domestic) risk-free rate (annualized return of 3%). The terminal value in U.S. dollars is:

$$\$26.8697 \text{ million} - \$670,640 = \$26.1991 \text{ million}$$

$$\frac{26.1991}{26.0000} - 1 = 0.0077 = 0.77\% \text{ gain}$$

In this scenario, using the currency hedge with the equity hedge resulted in a lower overall gain than just the equity hedge. The currency moved in the opposite direction than expected by the manager.

READING 33: RISK MANAGEMENT APPLICATIONS OF OPTION STRATEGIES

Time to complete: 11 hours

Reading summary: This reading focuses on applications of option strategies. Specifically, it has two parts. The first part is on equity options, where the candidates should know how to use covered calls and protective puts to manage risk exposure of individual shares. Additionally, the candidates need to compute and interpret payoff, profit, breakeven, and shapes of option strategies including bull spreads, bear spreads, butterfly spreads, option collars, straddles, and box spreads. The second part is on interest rate options. Candidates should know how to compute the effective annualized rate for a given interest rate outcome when a borrower or a lender manages the risk of an anticipated loan using interest rate options. Candidates should also know the payoffs of a series of interest rate outcomes when a floating rate loan is combined with an interest rate cap, an interest rate floor, or an interest rate collar. Additionally this reading covers option delta and gamma.

LESSON 1: OPTIONS STRATEGIES FOR EQUITY PORTFOLIOS

Candidates should master the following hedging and speculation strategies:

Equity options: compute and explain their value at expiration, maximum profit and loss, breakeven price, and explain their use in managing risk.

LOS 33a: Compare the use of covered calls and protective puts to manage risk exposure to individual securities. Vol 5, pp 286–292

OPTION STRATEGIES FOR EQUITY INVESTMENTS

This section focuses on option strategies that apply to stocks and stock indices; the following strategies are covered:

1. Covered calls;
2. Protective puts (insurance puts);
3. *Money spreads*: bull spreads, bear spreads, butterfly spreads;
4. *Combinations of calls and puts*: straddles, straps, strips, strangles, box spreads and collars.

For each of the strategies, the component structure, value at expiration, profit, maximum profit and maximum loss, and breakeven point(s) are determined.

The following notation applies:

S: The value of the underlying stock
X: The exercise price of an option
c: A call option premium
p: A put option premium
V: Value of a position
π: Profit of a transaction
r: Risk-free rate of interest
T: Option expiration
S^*_T: Breakeven (profit equals 0)

Covered Calls

A covered call is a portfolio of a share and a call option written on the share. When an investor writes a call option on a share that they own, the strategy is called a covered call and can be summarized as follows:

$$\text{Value at initiation} = V_0 = S_0 - c_0$$
$$\text{Value at option expiration} = V_T = S_T - c_T = S_T - \max(S_T - X, 0)$$
$$\text{Profit at option expiration} = V_T - V_0 = [S_T - \max(S_T - X, 0)] - [S_0 - c_0]$$
$$\text{Max profit} = X - [S_0 - c_0] \text{ when } S_T \geq X$$
$$\text{Max loss} = S_0 - c_0 \text{ when } S_T = 0$$
$$\text{Breakeven point} = S_T^* = S_0 - c_0$$

The following application exercise demonstrates the covered call strategy.

Example 1-1

An investor holds 100 shares of Apple Inc. stocks. The current stock price is $570 a share. He sells a call option contract on the stock. The call option has three months to maturity and an exercise price of $600. The call premium is $10 on a per share basis.

A. **Compute** the strategy's value at expiration and profit if three months later Apple stock is:
  i. $607 a share.
  ii. $582 a share.

B. **Compute** the maximum profit, maximum loss, and breakeven point.

Solutions:

A. i. When the terminal stock price is $607:

$$\text{Value at initiation} = V_0 = S_0 - c_0$$
$$= 570 - 10 = \$560$$
$$\text{Value at option expiration} = V_T = S_T - \max(S_T - X, 0)$$
$$= 607 - \max(607 - 600, 0) = \$600$$
$$\text{Profit at option expiration} = V_T - V_0$$
$$= 600 - 560 = \$40$$

ii. When the terminal stock price is $582:

$$\text{Value at initiation} = V_0 = S_0 - c_0$$
$$= 570 - 10 = \$560$$
$$\text{Value at option expiration} = V_T = S_T - \max(S_T - X, 0)$$
$$= 582 - \max(582 - 600, 0) = \$582$$
$$\text{Profit at option expiration} = V_T - V_0$$
$$= 582 - 560 = \$22$$

B. The covered call strategy has a maximum profit of $40 when the terminal stock price is $600 or higher. The covered call strategy has a maximum loss of $560 when the terminal stock price is $0. The breakeven point of the strategy is $560.

$$\text{Max profit} = X - [S_0 - c_0]$$
$$= 600 - 560 = \$40 \text{ when } S_T \geq X$$
$$\text{Max loss} = S_0 - c_0$$
$$= 570 - 10 = \$560 \text{ when } S_T = 0$$
$$\text{Breakeven point} = S_T^* = S_0 - c_0$$
$$= \$560$$

Protective Put

A protective put is also called an insurance put. It is a portfolio of a share and a long put option on the share. When an investor buys a put option on a share that they own, the strategy is called a protective put and can be summarized as follows:

$$\text{Value at initiation} = V_0 = S_0 - p_0$$
$$\text{Value at option expiration} = V_T = S_T + p_T = S_T + \max[X - S_T, 0)$$
$$\text{Profit at option expiration} = V_T - V_0 = [S_T + \max[X - S_T, 0)] - [S_0 + p_0]$$
$$\text{Max profit} = \infty \text{ when } S_T \text{ approaches } \infty$$
$$\text{Max loss} = [S_0 + p_0] - X \text{ when } S_T \leq X$$
$$\text{Breakeven point} = S_T^* = S_0 + p_0$$

The following application exercise demonstrates the protective put strategy.

Example 1-2

An investor holds 100 shares of Apple Inc. stocks. The current stock price is $600 a share. They buy a put option contract on the stock. The put option has three months to maturity and an exercise price of $575. The call premium is $30 on a per share basis.

- A. **Compute** the strategy's value at expiration and profit if three months later Apple stock is:
  - i. $627 a share.
  - ii. $549 a share.

- B. **Compute** the maximum profit, maximum loss, and breakeven point.

Solution:

- A. i. When the terminal stock price is $627:

  $$\text{Value at initiation} = V_0 = S_0 - p_0$$
  $$= 600 + 30 = \$630$$

  $$\text{Value at option expiration} = V_T = S_T + \max(X - S_T, 0)$$
  $$= 627 + \max(575 - 627, 0) = \$627$$

  $$\text{Profit at option expiration} = V_T - V_0$$
  $$= 627 - 630 = -\$3$$

  ii. When the terminal stock price is $549:

  $$\text{Value at initiation} = V_0 = S_0 - p_0$$
  $$= 600 + 30 = \$630$$

  $$\text{Value at option expiration} = V_T = S_T + \max(X - S_T, 0)$$
  $$= 549 + \max(575 - 549, 0) = \$575$$

  $$\text{Profit at option expiration} = V_T - V_0$$
  $$= 575 - 630 = -\$55$$

- B. The protective put strategy has a maximum profit of infinity when the terminal stock price approaches infinity. The protective put strategy has a maximum loss of $55 when the terminal stock price is at or below $575. The breakeven point of the strategy is $630.

  $$\text{Max profit} = \infty$$
  $$\text{Max loss} = [S_0 + p_0] - X$$
  $$= \$55 \text{ when } S_T < X$$
  $$\text{Breakeven point} = S_T^* = S_0 + p_0$$
  $$= \$630$$

LOS 33b: Calculate and interpret the value at expiration, profit, maximum profit, maximum loss, breakeven underlying price at expiration, and general shape of the graph for the following option strategies: bull spread, bear spread, butterfly spread, collar, straddle, box spread. Vol 5, pp 293–312

Money Spreads

An option spread is a portfolio of a long option and a short option. If the two options differ only in time to maturity, the option spread is called a time spread, horizontal spread, or calendar spread. If the two options differ only in exercise price, the option spread is called a money spread or vertical spread. This section focuses on money spreads, specifically examining three kinds of money spreads: bull spreads, bear spreads, and butterfly spreads.

Bull Spreads

A **bull spread** is an option money spread where an option is bought and an otherwise identical option but with a higher exercise price is sold. Note that both options share the same underlying asset and the same time to maturity. The only difference is that the long option has a lower exercise price and the short option has a higher exercise price. X_1 and X_2 denote the lower and higher exercise prices, respectively. A bull spread can be either $c_1 - c_2$ or $p_1 - p_2$. A trader buys a bull spread when he believes that the underlying stock price will go up.

A bull spread constructed using call options is summarized as follows:

$$\text{Value at initiation} = V_0 = c_1 - c_2$$

$$\text{Value at option expiration} = V_T = \max(S_T - X_1, 0) - \max(S_T - X_2, 0)$$

$$\text{Profit at option expiration} = V_T - V_0 = [\max(S_T - X_1, 0) - \max(S_T - X_2, 0)] - [c_1 - c_2]$$

$$\text{Max profit} = [X_2 - X_1] - [c_1 - c_2] \text{ when } S_T \geq X_2$$

$$\text{Max loss} = c_1 - c_2 \text{ when } S_T \leq X_1$$

$$\text{Breakeven point} = S_T^* = X_1 + [c_1 - c_2]$$

The following application exercise demonstrates a bull spread using call options.

Example 1-3

A trader pays $6 to buy a call with a strike price of $30, and collects $4 when he writes a call with the same underlying stock, the same maturity, and a different strike price of $35. Regarding the bull spread:

A. **Compute** the strategy's value at expiration and profit if, at expiration, the stock price is:
   i. $17 a share.
   ii. $33 a share.
   iii. $43 a share.

B. **Compute** the maximum profit, maximum loss, and breakeven point.

Solutions:

A.   i. When the terminal stock price is $17:

$$\text{Value at initiation} = V_0 = c_1 - c_2$$

$$= 6 - 4 = \$2$$

$$\text{Value at option expiration} = V_T = \max(S_T - X_1, 0) - \max(S_T - X_2, 0)$$

$$= \max(17 - 30, 0) - \max(17 - 35, 0) = \$0$$

$$\text{Profit at option expiration} = V_T - V_0 = [\max(S_T - X_1, 0)$$
$$- \max(S_T - X_2, 0)] - [c_1 - c_2]$$

$$= 0 - 2 = -\$2$$

   ii. When the terminal stock price is $33:

$$\text{Value at initiation} = V_0 = c_1 - c_2$$

$$= 6 - 4 = \$2$$

$$\text{Value at option expiration } V_T = \max(S_T - X_1, 0) - \max(S_T - X_2, 0)$$

$$= \max(33 - 30, 0) - \max(33 - 35, 0) = \$3$$

$$\text{Profit at option expiration} = V_T - V_0 = [\max(S_T - X_1, 0)$$
$$- \max(S_T - X_2, 0)] - [c_1 - c_2]$$

$$= 3 - 2 = \$1$$

   iii. When the terminal stock price is $43:

$$\text{Value at initiation} = V_0 = c_1 - c_2$$

$$= 6 - 4 = \$2$$

$$\text{Value at option expiration} = V_T = \max(S_T - X_1, 0) - \max(S_T - X_2, 0)$$

$$= \max(43 - 30, 0) - \max(43 - 35, 0) = \$5$$

$$\text{Profit at option expiration} = V_T - V_0 = [\max(S_T - X_1, 0)$$
$$- \max(S_T - X_2, 0)] - [c_1 - c_2]$$

$$= 5 - 2 = \$3$$

B.   The bull spread strategy has a maximum profit of $3 when the terminal stock price is at or above $35. The bull spread strategy has a maximum loss of $2 when the terminal stock price is at or below $30. The breakeven point of the strategy is $32.

$$\text{Max profit} = [X_2 - X_1] - [c_1 - c_2]$$
$$= [35 - 30] - [6 - 4] = \$3 \text{ when } S_T \geq 35$$

$$\text{Max loss} = c_1 - c_2$$
$$= 6 - 4 = \$2 \text{ when } S_T \leq 30$$

$$\text{Breakeven point} = S_T^* = X_1 + [c_1 - c_2]$$

$$= 30 + [6 - 4] = \$32$$

Bear Spreads

A **bear spread** is an option money spread where an option is bought and an otherwise identical option but with a lower exercise price is sold. Note that both options share the same underlying asset and the same time to maturity. The only difference is that the long option has a higher exercise price and the short option has a lower exercise price. A bear spread can be either $c_2 - c_1$ or $p_2 - p_1$. Note that the profit of a bear spread is exactly the mirror image of that of a bull spread. A bull spread and a corresponding bear spread form a zero-sum game. Put another way, if a trader sells a bull spread, the trade is equivalent to buying a bear spread. A trader buys a bear spread when he believes that the underlying stock price will go down.

A bear spread constructed using put options is summarized as follows:

$$\text{Value at initiation} = V_0 = p_2 - p_1$$
$$\text{Value at option expiration} = \max[X_2 - S_T, 0] - \max(X_1 - S_T, 0)$$
$$\text{Profit at option expiration} = V_T - V_0 = [\max(X_2 - S_T, 0) - \max(X_1 - S_T, 0)]$$
$$- [p_2 - p_1]$$
$$\text{Max profit} = [X_2 - X_1] - [p_2 - p_1] \text{ when } S_T \geq X_1$$
$$\text{Max loss} = p_2 - p_1 \text{ when } S_T \geq X_2$$
$$\text{Breakeven point} = S_T^* = X_2 - [p_2 - p_1]$$

The following application exercise demonstrates a bear spread using put options.

Example 1-4

A trader pays $9 to buy a put with a strike price of $60, and collects $3 when he writes a put with the same underlying stock, the same maturity, and a different strike price of $50. Regarding the bear spread:

  A. **Compute** the strategy's value at expiration and profit if, at expiration, the stock price is:
     i. $39 a share.
    ii. $52 a share.
   iii. $77 a share.

  B. **Compute** the maximum profit, maximum loss, and breakeven point.

Solutions:

  A. i. When the terminal stock price is $39:

$$\text{Value at initiation} = V_0 = p_2 - p_1$$
$$= 9 - 3 = \$6$$
$$\text{Value at option expiration} = V_T = \max(X_2 - S_T, 0) - \max(X_1 - S_T, 0)$$
$$= \max(60 - 39, 0) - \max(50 - 39, 0) = \$10$$
$$\text{Profit at option expiration} = V_T - V_0 = [\max(X_2 - S_T, 0)$$
$$- \max(X_1 - S_T, 0)] - [p_2 - p_1]$$
$$= 10 - 6 = -\$4$$

ii. When the terminal stock price is $52:

$$\text{Value at initiation} = V_0 = p_2 - p_1$$

$$= 9 - 3 = \$6$$

$$\text{Value at option expiration} = V_T = \max(X_2 - S_T, 0) - \max(X_1 - S_T, 0)$$

$$= \max(60 - 52, 0) - \max(50 - 52, 0) = \$8$$

$$\text{Profit at option expiration} = V_T - V_0 = [\max(X_2 - S_T, 0)$$
$$- \max(X_1 - S_T, 0)] - [p_2 - p_1]$$

$$= 8 - 6 = \$2$$

iii. When the terminal stock price is $77:

$$\text{Value at initiation} = V_0 = p_2 - p_1$$

$$= 9 - 3 = \$6$$

$$\text{Value at option expiration} = V_T = \max(X_2 - S_T, 0) - \max(X_1 - S_T, 0)$$

$$= \max(60 - 77, 0) - \max(50 - 77, 0) = \$0$$

$$\text{Profit at option expiration} = V_T - V_0 = [\max(X_2 - S_T, 0)$$
$$- \max(X_1 - S_T, 0)] - [p_2 - p_1]$$

$$= 0 - 6 = -\$6$$

B. The bear spread strategy has a maximum profit of $4 when the terminal stock price is at or below $50. The bear spread strategy has a maximum loss of $6 when the terminal stock price is at or above $60. The breakeven point of the strategy is $54.

$$\text{Max profit} = [X_2 - X_1] - [p_2 - p_1]$$

$$= [60 - 50] - [9 - 3] = \$4 \text{ when } S_T \leq 50$$

$$\text{Max loss} = p_2 - p_1$$

$$= 9 - 3 = \$6 \text{ when } S_T \geq X_2$$

$$\text{Breakeven point} = S_T^* = X_2 - [p_2 - p_1]$$

$$= 60 - [9 - 3] = \$54$$

Butterfly Spreads

A **butterfly spread** is a combination of three option positions of the same option class (call or put) with the same underlying asset and the same option time to maturity. The only difference is that these three options have different exercise prices, $X_1 < X_2 < X_3$, where $X_2 = (X_x + X_2) / 2$. A long butterfly spread involves buying one option with the lowest exercise price, buying one option with the highest exercise price, and selling two options with the middle exercise price. A butterfly spread can be either $c_1 - 2c_2 + c_3$ or $p_1 - 2p_2 + p_3$. A trader buys a butterfly spread when they believe that the underlying stock will not make a large price move and that the terminal stock price will be around the middle exercise price.

The properties of a butterfly spread using call options $c_1 - sc_2 + c_3$ are presented here. This butterfly spread using calls combines a long bull spread and a short bull spread (or bear spread). Similarly, a butterfly spread using puts should yield the same result if the options are correctly priced and it would combine a long and short bear spread.

$$\text{Value at initiation} = V_0 = c_1 - 2c_2 + c_3$$

$$\text{Value at option expiration} = V_T = \max(s_T - X_1, 0) - 2\max(S_T - X_2, 0) + \max(S_T - X_3, 0)$$

$$\text{Profit at option expiration} = V_T - V_0 = [\max[S_T - X_1, 0] - 2\max[S_T - X_2, 0] + \max(S_T - X_3, 0)] - [c_1 - 2c_2 + c_3]$$

$$\text{Max profit} = [X_2 - X_1] - [c_1 - 2c_2 + c_3] \text{ where } S_T = X_2$$

$$\text{Max loss} = c_1 - 2c_2 + c_3 \text{ when } S_T \geq X_3 \text{ or } S_T \leq X_1,$$

$$\text{Breakeven points} = S_T^* = X_1, + [c_1 - 2c_2 + c_3] \text{ and } 2X_2 - X_1, - [c_1 - 2c_2 + c_3]$$

Example 1-5

Stock A is currently worth $61 a share. A trader feels that it is unlikely that there will be a significant price move in the next six months; they construct a butterfly spread using call options. The market prices of six-month calls are given in the following table.

Strike Price	$55	$60	$65
Call Price	$10	$7	$5

A. **Compute** the strategy's value at expiration and profit if at expiration the stock price is:
   i. $37 a share.
   ii. $62 a share.
   iii. $73 a share.

B. **Compute** the maximum profit, maximum loss, and breakeven points.

Solutions:

A. i. When the terminal stock price is $37:

$$\text{Value at initiation} = V_0 = c_1 - 2c_2 + c_3 = \$1$$

$$\text{Value at option expiration} = V_T = \max(S_T - X_1, 0) - 2\max(S_T - X_2, 0) + \max(S_T - X_3, 0)$$

$$= \max(37 - 55, 0) - 2\max(37 - 60, 0) + \max(37 - 65, 0) = \$0$$

$$\text{Profit at option expiration} = V_T - V_0 = 0 - 1 = -\$1$$

ii. When the terminal stock price is $62:

$$\text{Value at initiation} = V_0 = c_1 - 2c_2 + c_3 = \$1$$

$$\text{Value at option expiration} = V_T = \max(S_T - X_1, 0) - 2\max(S_T - X_2, 0)$$
$$+ \max(S_T - X_3, 0)$$
$$= \max(62 - 55, 0) - 2\max(62 - 60, 0)$$
$$+ \max(62 - 65, 0) = \$3$$

$$\text{Profit at option expiration} = V_T - V_0 = 3 - 1 = \$2$$

iii. When the terminal stock price is $73:

$$\text{Value at initiation} = V_0 = c_1 - 2c_2 + c_3 = \$1$$

$$\text{Value at option expiration} = V_T = \max(S_T - X_1, 0) - 2\max(S_T - X_2, 0)$$
$$+ \max(S_T - X_3, 0)$$

$$= \max(73 - 55, 0) - 2\max(73 - 60, 0)$$
$$+ \max(73 - 65, 0) = \$0$$

$$\text{Profit at option expiration} = V_T - V_0 = 0 - 1 = -\$1$$

B. The butterfly spread strategy has a max profit of $4 when the terminal stock price is at the middle exercise price of $60. The butterfly spread strategy has a max loss of $1 when the terminal stock price is at or below $55 or at or above $65. The breakeven points of the strategy are $56 and $64.

$$\text{Max profit} = [X_2 - X_1] - [c_1 - 2c_2 + c_3]$$

$$= [60 - 55] - 1 = \$4 \text{ when } S_T = 60$$

$$\text{Max loss} = c_1 - 2c_2 + c_3$$

$$= \$1 \text{ when } S_T \geq 65 \text{ or } S_T \leq 55$$

$$\text{Breakeven points} = S_T^* = X_1 + [c_1 - 2c_2 + c_3]$$

$$= 55 + 1 = \$56$$
$$\text{and } 2X_2 - X_1 - [c_1 - 2c_2 + c_3]$$

$$= 65 - 1 = \$64$$

Combinations of Calls and Puts

Collars

An **option collar** is a portfolio of the underlying stock, a long put option on the stock (a protective put) and a short call option. Both options share the same underlying asset and the same option time to maturity. Consider a trader who holds a stock. They buy a put on the stock to form a protective put to eliminate the downside risk of the stock. The cost of the put option, however, can be significant. To reduce and even eliminate the cost of the put, they sell a call on the stock and use the call premium collected to reduce and even offset the cost of the put option. In a special case, called a zero-cost collar, they choose the exercise price of the call such that the call premium is exactly the same as the put premium. In this case, the collar is $= S_0 + p_1 - c_2$.

$$\text{Value at initiation} = V_0 = S_0 + [p_1 - c_2] = S_0 + 0 = S_0$$

$$\text{Value at option expiration} = V_T = S_T + \max(X_1 - S_T, 0) - \max(S_T - X_2, 0)$$

$$\text{Profit at option expiration} = V_T - V_0 = [S_T + \max(X_1 - S_T, 0)] - \max(S_T - X_2, 0) - [S_0]$$

$$\text{Max profit} = X_2 - S_0 \text{ when } S_T \geq X_2$$

$$\text{Max loss} = S_0 - X_1 \text{ when } S_T \leq X_1$$

$$\text{Breakeven points} = S_T^* = S_0$$

Example 1-6

A trader buys a stock at \$27 a share. Subsequently, he buys a put option on the stock with an exercise price of \$20, time to maturity of six months, and a premium of \$2.50. He also buys a call option with the exercise price of \$38 on the same underlying stock and same time to expiration; the premium is the same as the put, \$2.50. His portfolio is: $S_0 + p(X = 20) - c(X = 38)$. Regarding this option collar:

A. **Compute** the strategy's value at expiration and profit if in six months of time at expiration the stock price is:
   i. \$17 a share.
   ii. \$29 a share.
   iii. \$52 a share.

B. **Compute** the maximum profit, maximum loss, and breakeven point.

Solutions:

A. i. When the terminal stock price is \$17:

$$\text{Value of initiation} = V_0 = S_0 + [p_1 - c_2] = S_0 + 0 = \$27$$

$$\text{Value at option expiration} = V_T = S_T + \max(X_1 - S_T, 0) - \max(S_T - X_2, 0)$$

$$= 17 + \max(20 - 17, 0) - \max(17 - 38, 0) = \$20$$

$$\text{Profit at option expiration} = V_T - V_0 = 20 - 27 = -\$7$$

ii. When the terminal stock price is \$29:

$$\text{Value at initation} = V_0 = S + [p_1 - c_2] = S_0 + 0 = \$27$$

$$\text{Value at option expiration} = V_T = S_T + \max(X_1 - S_T, 0) - \max(S_T - X_2, 0)$$

$$= 29 + \max(20 - 29, 0) - \max(29 - 38, 0) = \$29$$

$$\text{Profit at option expiration} = V_T - V_0 = 29 - 27 = \$2$$

iii. When the terminal stock price is $52:

$$\text{Value of initiation} = V_0 = S_0 + [\, p_1 - c_2\,] = S_0 + 0 = \$27$$

$$\text{Value at option expiration} = V_T = S_T + \max(X_1 - S_T, 0)$$
$$- \max(S_T - X_2, 0)$$

$$= 52 + \max(20 - 52, 0) - \max(52 - 38, 0) = \$38$$

$$\text{Profit at option expiration} = V_T - V_0 = 38 - 27 = \$11$$

B. The collar strategy has a maximum profit of $11 when the terminal stock price is at or above $38. The collar strategy has a maximum loss of $7 when the terminal stock price is at or below $20. The breakeven point of the strategy is $27.

$$\text{Max profit} = X_2 = S_0$$
$$= 38 - 27 = \$11 \text{ when } S_T \geq X_2$$
$$\text{Max loss} = S_0 - X_1$$
$$= 27 - 20 = -\$7 \text{ when } S_T \leq X_1$$
$$\text{Breakeven point} = S_T^* = S_0 = \$27$$

Straddles

An **option straddle** is a portfolio of two options, a long call and a long put option on the same underlying stock with the same exercise price and same time to maturity. A straddle is: $c + p$. A trader buys a straddle when he believes that the underlying stock will make a large price move, but he is not sure which side (up or down) the stock will move.

$$\text{Value at initiation} = V_0 = c_0 + p_0$$

$$\text{Value at option expiration} = V_T = \max(S_T - X, 0) + \max(X - S_T, 0)$$

$$\text{Profit at option expiration} = V_T - V_0 = [\max(S_T - X, 0)] + \max(X - S_T, 0) - [c_0 + p_0]$$

$$\text{Max profit} = \infty \text{ when } S_T \to \infty$$

$$\text{Max loss} = c_0 + p_0 \text{ when } S_T = X$$

$$\text{Breakeven point} = S_T^* = X + [c_0 + p_0] \text{ and } X - [c_0 + p_0]$$

Example 1-7

A trader buys a call option and a put option on the same stock. Both options have the same exercise price of $95 and same time to maturity of three months. The call and put option premiums are $9 and $7, respectively. His portfolio is $c(X = 95) + p(X = 95)$. Regarding this option straddle:

A. **Compute** the strategy's value at expiration and profit if in three months at expiration the stock price is:
   i. $70 a share.
   ii. $93 a share.
   iii. $155 a share.

B. **Compute** the maximum profit, maximum loss, and breakeven points.

Solutions:

A. i. When the terminal stock price is $70:

$$\text{Value at initiation} = V_0 = c_0 + p_0 = 9 + 7 = \$16$$
$$\text{Value at option expiration} = V_T = \max(S_T - X, 0) + \max(X - S_T, 0)$$
$$= \max(70 - 95, 0) + \max(95 - 70, 0 = \$25$$
$$\text{Profit at option expiration} = V_T - V_0 = 25 - 16 = \$9$$

ii. When the terminal stock price is $93:

$$\text{Value at initiation} = V_0 + c_0 + p_0 = 9 + 7 = \$16$$
$$\text{Value at option expiration} = V_T = \max(S_T - X, 0) + \max(X - S_T, 0)$$
$$= \max(93 - 95, 0) + \max(95 - 93, 0) = \$2$$
$$\text{Profit at option expiration} = V_T - V_0 = 2 - 16 = -\$14$$

iii. When the terminal stock price is $155:

$$\text{Value at initiation} = V_0 = c_0 + p_0 = 9 + 7 = \$16$$
$$\text{Value at option expiration} = V_T = \max(S_T - X, 0) + \max(X - S_T, 0)$$
$$= \max(155 - 95, 0) + \max(95 - 155, 0) = \$60$$
$$\text{Profit at option expiration} = V_T - V_0 = 60 - 16 = \$44$$

B. The straddle strategy has an unlimited maximum profit when the terminal stock price is sufficiently high. The straddle strategy has a maximum loss of $16 when the terminal stock price is at $95. The breakeven points of the strategy are $111 and $79.

$$\text{Max profit} = \infty \text{ when } S_T \to \infty$$
$$\text{Max loss} = c_0 + p_0 = \$16 \text{ when } S_T = \$95$$
$$\text{Breakeven points} = S_T^* = X + [c_0 + p_0]$$
$$= 95 + 16 = \$111 \text{ and } X - [c + p_0]$$
$$= 95 - 16 = \$79$$

Straps, Strips, and Strangles

An **option strap** is a portfolio of two option positions: two long calls and one long put option on the same underlying stock with the same exercise price and same time to maturity. It is basically adding a call to a straddle. A strap is $2c + p$. A trader buys a strap when he believes that the underlying stock will make a large price move; although they are not sure which direction the stock price will move, they believe that it is more likely to move up than down.

An **option strip** is a portfolio of two option positions: one long call and two long put options on the same underlying stock with the same exercise price and same time to maturity. It is basically adding a put to a straddle. A strip is $c + 2p$. A trader buys a strip when she believes that the underlying stock will make a large price move; although she is not sure which direction the stock price will move, she believes that it is more likely to move down than up.

An **option strangle** is a portfolio of two option positions: one long call and a long put options on the same underlying stock with different exercise prices and same time to maturity. It is basically a variation of a straddle. A strangle is $c + p$. A trader buys a strangle when she believes that the underlying stock will make a large price move; although she is not sure which direction the stock price will move.

Box Spread

An **option box spread** is a portfolio of four option positions: a long bull spread with call options and a short bull spread (bear spread) with put options. All four options share the same underlying stock and the same time to maturity. A box spread is $(c_1 - c_2 + p_2 - p_1)$. A trader buys a box spread to lock in a fixed terminal value of $(X_1 - X_2)$. The box spread portfolio is a synthetic risk-free bond. Traders use box spreads to explore arbitrage opportunities, when option prices are not correctly set.

$$\text{Value at initiation} = V_0 = [c_1 - c_2] + [p_2 - p_1]$$
$$\text{Value at option expiration} = V_T = X_2 - X_1$$
$$\text{Profit at option expiration} = V_T - V_0 = [X_2 - X_1] - [[c_1 - c_2] + [p_2 - p_1]]$$
$$\text{Max profit} = \text{Profit} = [X_2 - X_1] - [[c_1 - c_2] + [p_2 - p_1]]$$
$$\text{regardless of terminal stock price}$$
$$\text{Max loss} = \text{None}$$
$$\text{Breakeven point} = \text{None}$$

Example 1-8

A trader buys a box spread using the four options listed below; option exercise prices and option premiums are given. All options share the same underlying stock and the same time to maturity of 39 days. The trader's portfolio is $[c(X = 1,325) - c(X = 1,425)] + p(X = 1,425) - p(X = 1,325)]$. The risk-free rate is 5%. Regarding this box spread:

Option Price	Call	Put
$X_1 = \$1,325$	$111.125	$10.25
$X_2 = \$1,425$	$37.75	$35

A. **Compute** the strategy's value at expiration and profit if in 39 days at the options expiration, the box spread pays off $[X_2 - X_1] = \$100$, regardless of the terminal stock price.

B. Compute maximum profit, maximum loss, and breakeven point.

C. Determine if the box spread pricing presents an attractive opportunity.

Solutions:

A. If the trader holds the box spread until maturity, then the payoff is $100, regardless of the terminal stock price. The initial cash outflow of the strategy is $98.125.

$$\text{Value at initiation} = V_0 = [c_1 - c_2] + [p_2 - p_1]$$

$$= [111.125 - 37.75] - [35 - 10.25] = \$98.125$$

$$\text{Value at option expiration} = V_T = X_2 - X_1$$

$$= 1,425 - 1,325 = \$100$$

$$\text{Profit at option expiration} = V_T - V_0 = 100 - 98.125 = \$1.875$$

B. The box spread strategy has a fixed profit of $1.875 regardless of the level of terminal stock price. The box spread strategy does not generate losses because it is a synthetic risk-free bond. There are no breakeven points of the strategy.

$$\text{Max profit} = 100 - 98.125 = \$1.875 \text{ at all } S_T$$

$$\text{Max loss} = \text{None}$$

$$\text{Breakeven point} = \text{None}$$

C. Based on the risk-free rate of 5%, when the options expire in 39 days, the box spread should be worth $99.48, generating an instant gain in value of $1.36.

$$\frac{(X_2 - X_1)}{(1+r)^T} = 100 / (1.05)^{\frac{39}{365}} = \$99.48$$

$$\$99.48 - 98.125 = \$1.36$$

LESSON 2: INTEREST RATE OPTION STRATEGIES

Candidates should master the following hedging and speculation strategies:

Interest rate options: calculate appropriate payoffs for various outcomes

LOS 33c: Calculate the effective annual rate for a given interest rate outcome when a borrower (lender) manages the risk of an anticipated loan using an interest rate call (put) option. Vol 5, pp 313–323

INTEREST RATE OPTION STRATEGIES

This section examines interest rate options and their applications. Interest rate options include call options and put options. They are options on interest rates, mostly likely LIBOR rates. These options generate a positive payoff when the realized underlying interest rate is higher (for a call option) or lower (for a put option) than the option's exercise rate, which is preset in the option contract. One unique and important feature of interest rate options is that the payoff of the option does not occur at the option's expiration. Instead, payoff of the option is paid by the option seller (writer) to the option buyer one time period after the option expiration. The reason is clear once you understand the nature of the interest rate options. In a very simplistic way, interest rates measure the speed of money acquiring interest (or time value of money). Note that money does not acquire interest over an instant. The act of acquiring interest is completed over time. Consequently, the impact of a difference in interest rates (i.e., the difference between a realized spot interest rate and contract preset exercise rate) is not materialized until one time period after the option's expiration. Given the option payoff is paid exactly at that time (one time period after the option expiration), hedging or speculation goals are successfully achieved.

The payoff of an interest rate call option, to be paid one time period after option expiration, is given below:

$$\text{Call option payoff} = \text{Notional principal} \times \max(\text{Realized spot rate} - \text{Exercise rate}, 0)$$
$$\times \frac{\text{Days in underlying rate}}{360}$$

The payoff of an interest rate put option, to be paid one time period after option expiration, is given below:

$$\text{Put option payoff} = \text{Notional principal} \times \max(\text{Exercise rate} - \text{Realized spot rate}, 0)$$
$$\times \frac{\text{Days in underlying rate}}{360}$$

LOS 33d: Calculate the payoffs for a series of interest rate outcomes when a floating rate loan is combined with 1) an interest rate cap, 2) an interest rate floor, or 3) an interest rate collar. Vol 5, pp 323–333

Applications of an Interest Rate Call Option

An **interest rate call option** can be used to hedge the risk of hiking interest rate when an institution intends to borrow in the future.

Consider the following scenario:

- On April 10, a corporation decides to borrow $50 million on August 10 for 180 days.
- The cost of short-term borrowing of the firm is LIBOR + 200 basis points; the spot LIBOR rate is 5.3 percent.
- The treasurer is concerned about a potential increase in LIBOR rates between April 10 and August 10. After talking with risk managers, the treasurer decides to purchase an interest rate call on a 180-day LIBOR with a maturity on August 10 and a notional principal of $50 million. The exercise rate of the interest rate call is 4.9 percent. The cost of the interest rate call is 0.5 percent of the notional, or $250,000.
- Note that the option premium is paid on April 10 and that the option expires on August 10. Also note that the potential interest rate call payoff is paid not at the option expiration of August 10, but it is paid one period, 180 days, after the option expiration.

Here is the analysis on the effective rate of borrowing of the firm after considering the cost of interest rate call.

Two possible cases of LIBOR rate on August 10 are considered:

1. Realized LIBOR is 3.9 percent on August 10.
2. Realized LIBOR is 6.3 percent on August 10.

Analysis of the first case: Realized LIBOR is 3.9 percent on August 10.

1. There are 122 days between April 10 and August 10. Given that the interest rate call option premium must be paid on April 10, the future value of the option premium on August 10 is:

$$250,000 \times \left(1 + (0.053 + 0.02) \times \frac{122}{360}\right) = \$256,185$$

2. On August 10, if the realized spot 180-day LIBOR rate is 3.9 percent, the interest rate call finishes out-of-the-money and there is no payoff from the call. The firm borrows at 3.9 percent. Net cash flow on August 10 is the difference between $50 million and the future value of the option premium.

$$50,000,000 - 256,185 = \$49,743,815$$

3. After 180 days from August 10, the firm pays creditors the future value of the loan:

$$\text{Call option payoff} = 50,000,000 \times \max(0.039 - 0.049, 0) \times \frac{180}{360} = \$0$$

$$50,000,000 \times \left(1 + (0.039 + 0.02) \times \frac{180}{360}\right) = \$51,475,000.$$

4. The effective annualized rate of loan is:

$$\left(\frac{51,475,000}{49,743,815}\right)^{365/180} - 1 = 7.1833\%$$

Analysis of the second case: Realized LIBOR is 6.3 percent on August 10.

1. There are 122 days between April 10 and August 10. Given that the interest rate call option premium must be paid on April 10, the future value of the option premium on August 10 is:

$$250,000 \times \left(1 + (0.053 + 0.02) \times \frac{122}{360}\right) = \$256,185$$

2. On August 10, if the realized spot 180-day LIBOR rate is 6.3 percent, the interest rate call finishes in-the-money and there is positive payoff from the call 180 days after August 10. The firm borrows at 6.3 percent. Net cash flow on August 10 is the difference between $50 million and the future value of the option premium.

$$50,000,000 - 256,185 = \$49,743,815$$

3. After 180 days from August 10, the firm collects the payoff from the interest rate call option and pays creditors the future value of the loan:

$$\text{Call option payoff} = 50{,}000{,}000 \times \max(0.063 - 0.049, 0) \times \frac{180}{360} = \$350{,}000$$

$$50{,}000{,}000 \times \left(1 + (0.063 + 0.02) \times \frac{180}{360}\right) = \$52{,}075{,}000$$

$$52{,}075{,}000 - 350{,}000 = \$51{,}725{,}000$$

4. The effective annualized rate of loan is:

$$\left(\frac{51{,}725{,}000}{49{,}743{,}815}\right)^{365/180} - 1 = 8.2415\%$$

Note that the effective annualized rate stays at the above 8.2415 percent for any realized LIBOR rate beyond the option exercise rate of 4.9 percent.

Applications of an Interest Rate Put Option

An **interest rate put option** can be used to hedge the risk of decreases in interest rate when an institution intends to lend in the future.

Consider the following scenario:

- On February 10, a bank signs a contract to lend $20 million to one of its clients on May 10 for 90 days.
- The lending rate is the spot 90-day LIBOR rate on May 10 plus 250 basis points; the spot LIBOR rate is 3.8 percent.
- The treasurer is concerned about a potential decrease in LIBOR rates between February 10 and May 10. They decide to purchase an interest rate put on a 90-day LIBOR with a maturity on May 10 and a notional principal of $20 million. The exercise rate of the interest rate put is 4.1 percent. The cost of the interest rate call is 0.5 percent of the notional, or $100,000.
- Note that the option premium is paid on February 10 and that the option expires on May 10. Also note that the potential interest rate put payoff is paid not at the option expiration of May 10, but it is paid one period, 90 days after the option expiration.

Here is the analysis on the effective rate of lending of the bank after considering the cost of interest rate put.

Two possible cases of LIBOR rate on May 10 are considered:

1. Realized LIBOR is 2.4 percent on May 10.
2. Realized LIBOR is 5.8 percent on May 10.

Analysis of the first case: Realized LIBOR is 2.4 percent on May 10.

1. There are 89 days between February 10 and May 10. Given that the interest rate put option premium must be paid on February 10, the future value of the option premium on May 10 is:

$$100,000 \times \left(1 + (0.038 + 0.025) \times \frac{89}{360}\right) = \$101,558$$

2. On May 10, if the realized spot 90-day LIBOR rate is 2.4 percent, the interest rate put finishes in-the-money and there is positive payoff from the put 90 days after May 10. The bank lends to its client at 2.4 percent. Net cash flow on May 10 is the sum between the $20 million loan and the future value of the option premium.

$$20,000,000 + 101,558 = \$20,101,558$$

3. After 90 days from May 10, the firm collects the client principal plus interest as well as the put option payoff:

$$\text{Put option payoff} = 20,000,000 \times \max(0.041 - 0.024, 0) \times \frac{90}{360} = \$85,000$$

$$20,000,000 \times \left(1 + (0.024 + 0.025) \times \frac{90}{360}\right) = \$20,245,000$$

$$20,245,000 + 85,000 = \$20,330,000$$

4. The effective annualized rate of loan is:

$$\left(\frac{20,330,000}{20,101,558}\right)^{365/90} - 1 = 4.6895\%$$

Note that the effective annualized rate stays at the above 4.6895 percent for any realized LIBOR rate below the option exercise rate of 4.1 percent.

Analysis of the second case: Realized LIBOR is 5.8 percent on May 10.

1. There are 89 days between February 10 and May 10. Given that the interest rate put option premium must be paid on February 10, the future value of the option premium on May 10 is:

$$100,000 \times \left(1 + (0.038 + 0.025) \times \frac{89}{360}\right) = \$101,558$$

2. On May 10, if the realized spot 90-day LIBOR rate is 5.8 percent, the interest rate put finishes out-of-the-money and there is zero payoff from the put option. The bank lends to its client at 5.8 percent. Net cash flow on May 10 is the sum between $20 million loan and the future value of the option premium.

$$20,000,000 + 101,558 = \$20,101,558$$

3. After 90 days from May 10, the firm collects the client principal plus interest:

$$\text{Put option payoff} = 20,000,000 \times \max(0.041 - 0.058, 0) \times \frac{90}{360} = \$0$$

$$20,000,000 \times \left(1 + (0.058 + 0.025) \times \frac{90}{360}\right) = \$20,415,000$$

4. The effective annualized rate of loan is:

$$\left(\frac{20,415,000}{20,101,558}\right)^{365/90} - 1 = 6.4761\%$$

Applications of an Interest Rate Cap

An **interest rate cap** is a portfolio of caplets, which are a sequence of interest rate call options on the underlying interest rate, most likely LIBOR. An interest rate cap has an exercise rate, which applies to all caplets. Each caplet in the cap has an expiration. Putting all expirations together, they cover the cap settlement dates during the life of the cap. Note that because a caplet is a call option on the underlying interest rate, the payoff of a caplet is delivered one time period after the expiration of the caplet.

An interest rate cap can be used to hedge the risk of hiking interest rate when an institution intends to issue floating-rate bonds in the future (or after an institution issues a floating-rate bond). Because the institution pays interest on the floating-rate bond, increases in reference benchmark interest rate increases the institution's cost of debt, a risk factor that the institution may wish to hedge.

Consider the following scenario:

- On April 10, 2020, a corporation issues a three-year floating-rate debt with $40 million face value.
- The floating rate is LIBOR plus 200 basis points. Interest payments are settled semiannually (October 10, 2020, April 10, 2021, October 10, 2021, April 10, 2022, and so on). Interest payments are computed based on the exact number of days in an interest accruing period. The spot 180-day LIBOR rate is 2.8 percent on April 10, 2020.
- Risk managers in the firm are concerned about the possibility that LIBOR rate may increase significantly over the next three years, making the cost of financing the firm's floating-rate debt expensive. To hedge the risk of hiking interest rate, the firm decides to buy an interest rate cap.
- The interest rate cap has an exercise rate of 3.2 percent and a notional principal of $40 million, matching the size of the floating-rate bond issue. The interest rate cap has three years to maturity with semiannual settlements. Note that the interest rate cap is made up of five caplets, and not six caplets. The premium of the interest rate cap is 0.4 percent of the notional $40 million, or $160,000, to be paid on April 10, 2020.

The following table details all transactions.

- Column 1 lists the bond issue day (4/10/2020) and all six coupon-paying dates during the life of the bond.
- Column 2 lists the realized spot six-month LIBOR rate, which is the reference rate based on which floating-rate interest payments are computed.
- Column 3 computes the numbers of days between two coupon payment dates. The numbers of days between coupon-paying dates are used to compute the amount of floating-rate interest due.
- Column 4 lists the loan rates, which is the benchmark six-month LIBOR rate plus the interest rate spread of 200 basis points. They are directly derived from the second column.
- Column 5 computes the dollar amount of interest due, based on $40 million face value, loan rate at previous settlement date, and the number of days between previous settlement date and the current date.
- Column 6 lists the payoffs of the interest rate cap. Note that (1) Column 6 lists the size and timing of the payoff of the interest rate cap. (2) The cash flow of a caplet is delivered one time period after the caplet expires. (3) Given that the floating rate bond has a time to maturity of three years and that the coupon payments are made semiannually, there are combined six coupon payments. However, there is no uncertainty in the size of the first coupon payment because it is based on the spot rate on 4/10/2020, the day when the bond is first issued. The rate is observable on 4/10/2020 and there is no need and no way to hedge a realized known variable because there is no uncertainty attached to the realization. Consequently, there are only five days when unknown spot six-month LIBOR rates are used to determine floating-rate interest payments. Consequently, to hedge the risk in spot LIBOR rates on these five days, only five caplets are needed, one for each day to set interest payments. The five dates are October 10, 2020, April 10, 2021, October 10, 2021, April 10, 2022, and October 10, 2022. These are exactly five days when corresponding five caplets expire. Payoffs of the caplets will be delivered one period (six months) after the caplet expirations. Column 6 of the following table clearly presents payoffs of caplets.
- Column 7 provides the effective interest payment after incorporating caplet payoffs. It is the difference between column 5 and column 6.

1	2	3	4	5	6	7
Date	Spot Rate	# Days	Loan Rate	Interest Due	Caplet Payoff	Effective Interest
4/10/2020	2.80%	183	4.80%			
10/10/2020	3.40%	182	5.40%	$ 976,000		$ 976,000
4/10/2021	3.10%	183	5.10%	$1,092,000	$ 40,444	$1,051,556
10/10/2021	3.50%	182	5.50%	$1,037,000	$ 0	$1,037,000
4/10/2022	3.70%	183	5.70%	$1,112,222	$ 60,667	$1,051,556
10/10/2022	3.80%	182	5.80%	$1,159,000	$101,667	$1,057,333
4/10/2023	3.90%			$1,172,889	$121,333	$1,051,556

Here is the analysis of the example using numbers.

On 4/10/2020, the three-year floating bond is issued. The spot LIBOR rate of 2.80 percent on 4/10/2020 determines the floating rate coupon interest payment on the next coupon-paying day, 10/10/2020. There are 183 days between 4/10/2020 and 10/10/2020 and the interest due is based on LIBOR plus 200 basis points.

$$\text{Interest due on October 10, 2020} = 40,000,000 \times (0.028 + 0.02) \times \frac{183}{360} = \$976,000$$

On 10/10/2020, the spot LIBOR rate turns out to be 3.40 percent.

$$\text{Interest due on April 10, 2021} = 40,000,000 \times (0.034 + 0.02) \times \frac{182}{360} = \$1,092,000$$

The first caplet expires on 10/10/2020.

$$\text{First caplet payoff} = 40,000,000 \times max(3.40\% - 3.20\%, 0) \times \frac{182}{360} = \$40,444$$

Note that even though the first caplet expires on 10/10/2020, the payoff of $40,444 is not paid until 182 days later on the next coupon payment day of 4/10/2021. As a result the effective interest payment of $976,000 is paid to bondholders on 10/10/2020.

On 04/10/2021, effective interest payment due is:

$$\text{Effective interest due on April 10, 2021} = 1,092,000 - 40,444 = \$1,051,556$$

On 04/10/2021, the spot LIBOR rate turns out to be 3.10 percent.

$$\text{Interest due on October 10, 2021} = 40,000,000 \times (0.031 + 0.02) \times \frac{183}{360}$$
$$= \$1,037,000$$

The second caplet expires on 04/10/2021.

$$\text{Second caplet payoff} = 40,000,000 \times max(3.10\% - 3.20\%, 0) \times \frac{183}{360} = \$0$$

On 10/10/2021, effective interest payment due is:

$$\text{Effective interest due on October } 10,2021 = 1{,}037{,}000 - 0 = \$1{,}037{,}000$$

The procedure is repeated at each coupon-paying day until the bond matures. Note that there are only five caplets and not six caplets. The preceding table summarizes all transactions.

Applications of an Interest Rate Floor

An **interest rate floor** is a portfolio of floorlets, which are a sequence of interest rate put options on the underlying interest rate, most likely LIBOR. An interest rate floor has an exercise rate, which applies to all floorlets. Each floorlet in the floor has an expiration. Putting all expirations together, they cover the floor settlement dates during the life of the floor. Note that because a floorlet is a put option on the underlying interest rate, the payoff of a floorlet is delivered one time period after the expiration of the floorlet.

An interest rate floor can be used to hedge the risk of decreasing interest rate when an institution intends to buy floating-rate bonds in the future (or after an institution buys a floating-rate bond). Because the institution receives interest on the floating-rate bond, decreases in reference benchmark interest rate decrease the institution's interest income, a risk factor that the institution may wish to hedge.

Consider the following scenario:

- On April 10, 2020, a portfolio manager purchases a newly issued three-year floating-rate debt with $100 million face value.
- The floating rate is LIBOR plus 100 basis points. Interest payments are settled semiannually (October 10, 2020, April 10, 2021, October 10, 2021, April 10, 2022, and so on). Interest payments are computed based on the exact number of days in an interest accruing period. The spot 180-day LIBOR rate is 3.8 percent on April 10, 2020.
- The portfolio manager is concerned about the possibility that LIBOR rate may decrease significantly over the next three years, making the interest income to the fund low. To hedge the risk of decrease in interest rate, the fund manager decides to buy an interest rate floor.
- The interest rate floor has an exercise rate of 3.6 percent and a notional principal of $100 million, matching the size of the floating rate bond holdings in the fund. The interest rate floor has three years to maturity with semiannual settlements. Note that the interest rate floor is made up of five floorlets, and not six floorlets. The premium of the interest rate floor is 0.6 percent of the notional $100 million, or $600,000, to be paid on April 10, 2020.

The following table details all transactions.

- Column 1 lists the bond purchase day (4/10/2020) and all six coupon-paying dates during the life of the bond.
- Column 2 lists the realized spot six-month LIBOR rate, which is the reference rate based on which floating-rate interest payments are computed.

- Column 3 computes the numbers of days between two coupon payment dates. The numbers of days between coupon-paying dates are used to compute the amount of floating rate interest income to the portfolio manager.
- Column 4 lists the loan rates, which is the benchmark six-month LIBOR rate plus the interest rate spread of 100 basis points. They are directly derived from the second column.
- Column 5 computes the dollar amount of interest income, based on $100 million face value, loan rate at previous settlement date, and the number of days between previous settlement date and the current date.
- Column 6 lists the payoffs of the interest rate floor. The cash flow of a floorlet is delivered one time period after the floorlet expires. Given that the floating-rate bond has a time to maturity of three years and that the coupon payments are made semiannually, there are combined six coupon payments and five floorlets. Column 6 of the following table clearly presents payoffs of floorlets.
- Column 7 provides the effective interest income after incorporating floorlet payoffs. It is the sum of column 5 and column 6.

1	2	3	4	5	6	7
Date	Spot Rate	# Days	Loan Rate	Interest Due	Floorlet Payoff	Effective Interest
4/10/2020	3.80%	183	4.80%			
10/10/2020	3.40%	182	4.40%	$2,440,000		$2,440,000
4/10/2021	3.10%	183	4.10%	$2,224,444	$101,111	$2,325,556
10/10/2021	3.70%	182	4.70%	$2,084,167	$254,167	$2,338,333
4/10/2022	3.40%	183	4.40%	$2,376,111	$ 0	$2,376,111
10/10/2022	3.60%	182	4.60%	$2,236,667	$101,667	$2,338,333
4/10/2023	3.90%			$2,325,556	$ 0	$2,325,556

Here is the analysis of the example using numbers.

On 4/10/2020, the three-year floating bond is purchased. The spot LIBOR rate of 3.80 percent on 4/10/2020 determines the floating-rate coupon interest income on the next coupon paying day, 10/10/2020. There are 183 days between 4/10/2020 and 10/10/2020 and the interest due is based on LIBOR plus 100 basis points.

$$\text{Interest income on October 10, 2020} = 100,000,000 \times (0.038 + 0.01) \times \frac{183}{360}$$
$$= \$2,440,000$$

On 10/10/2020, the spot LIBOR rate turns out to be 3.40 percent.

$$\text{Interest income on April 10, 2021} = 100,000,000 \times (0.034 + 0.01) \times \frac{182}{360}$$
$$= \$2,224,444$$

The first floorlet expires on 10/10/2020.

$$\text{First floorlet payoff} = 100,000,000 \times max(3.60\% - 3.40\%, 0) \times \frac{182}{360} = \$101,111$$

Note that even though the first floorlet expires on 10/10/2020, the payoff of $101,111 is not paid until 182 days later on the next coupon payment day of 4/10/2021. As a result, the portfolio manager receives interest income of $2,440,000 on 10/10/2020.

On 04/10/2021, effective interest income is:

$$\text{Effective interest income on April } 10, 2021 = 2,224,444 + 101,111 = \$2,335,556$$

On 04/10/2021, the spot LIBOR rate turns out to be 3.10 percent.

$$\text{Interest income on October } 10, 2021 = 100,000,000 \times (0.031 + 0.01) \times \frac{183}{360}$$
$$= \$2,084,157$$

The second floorlet expires 04/10/2021.

$$\text{Second floorlet payoff} = 100,000,000 \times max(3.60\% - 3.10\%, 0) \times \frac{183}{360}$$
$$= \$254,167$$

On 10/10/2021, effective interest income is:

$$\text{Effective interest income on October } 10, \ 2021 = 2,084,167 + 254,167$$
$$= \$2,338,333$$

The procedure is repeated at each coupon-paying day until the bond matures. Note that there are only five floorlets and not six floorlets. The preceding table summarizes all transactions.

Applications of an Interest Rate Collar

This section combines interest rate caps and floors to create an **interest rate collar**. Recall in equity option trading strategies the discussion of option collars. The same concept is applied to interest rate options and interest rate collars. An interest rate collar is a portfolio of a long interest rate cap and a short interest rate floor.

An interest rate cap pays off when the underlying (LIBOR) rate is above the cap's exercise rate. An interest rate floor pays off when the underlying (LIBOR) rate is below the floor's exercise rate.

A floating-rate bond issuer pays coupon interest based on a floating rate pegged to the LIBOR rate. The bond issues may purchase an interest rate collar, by buying an interest rate cap to hedge away the risk of increase in LIBOR rate and by selling an interest rate floor to use the option premium of the interest rate floor to reduce (offset) the cost (option premium) of the interest rate cap. After the interest rate cap position is set up, the floating-rate bond issuer pays an effective benchmark rate (in addition to a spread) that falls between the exercise rate of the interest rate floor and the interest rate cap. If the option premium of the interest rate cap is exactly offset by the option premium of the interest rate floor, the interest rate collar is called a zero-cost interest rate collar.

The following numerical example demonstrates an application of interest rate collar.

- On April 10, 2020, a corporation issues a three-year floating-rate bond with $60 million face value.
- The floating rate is LIBOR plus 50 basis points. Interest payments are settled semiannually (October 10, 2020, April 10, 2021, October 10, 2021, April 10, 2012, and so on). Interest payments are computed based on the exact number of days in an interest accruing period. The spot 180-day LIBOR rate is 3.8 percent on April 10, 2020.
- Risk managers in the firm are concerned about the possibility that LIBOR rate may increase significantly over the next three years, making the cost of financing the firm's floating rate debt expensive.
- To hedge the risk of hiking interest rate and to minimize the net out-of-pocket hedging cost, the firm decides to buy a zero-cost interest rate collar, where the exercise rate of the interest rate cap exercise is set at 4.5 percent and the exercise rate of the interest rate floor is 3.4 percent. The interest rate cap and the interest rate floor share the same notional principal of $60 million. They have the same three years to maturity with semiannual settlements. There are five caplets in the cap and five floorlets in the floor.

Note that the firm pays its bondholders at the rate of LIBOR plus 50 basis points. Additionally, when the LIBOR rate is higher than the exercise rate of the cap of 4.5 percent, the interest rate cap pays off. The payoffs are just enough to wipe out any interest payment in excess of the amount that corresponds to 4.5 percent of LIBOR. Consequently, the difference between the interest payment and the interest rate cap payoff is exactly equal to the interest payment corresponding to a LIBOR rate of 4.5 percent.

When the LIBOR rate is lower than the exercise rate of the floor of 3.4 percent, the firm has to make payments to the interest rate floor buyer (note that the firm is the interest rate floor seller), so that the sum of interest payment to bondholders and the payment of interest rate floor is exactly equal to the interest payment corresponding to a LIBOR rate of 3.4 percent.

Date	Spot Rate	# Days	Loan Rate	Interest Due	Caplet Payoff	Floorlet Payoff	Effective Interest
4/10/2020	3.80%	183	4.30%				
10/10/2020	4.90%	182	5.40%	$1,311,500			$1,311,500
4/10/2021	4.60%	183	5.10%	$1,638,000	$121,333	$ 0	$1,516,667
10/10/2021	3.90%	182	4.40%	$1,555,500	$ 30,500	$ 0	$1,525,000
4/10/2022	3.10%	183	3.60%	$1,334,667	$ 0	$ 0	$1,334,667
10/10/2022	3.20%	182	3.70%	$1,098,000	$ 0	$91,500	$1,189,500
4/10/2023	3.70%			$1,122,333	$ 0	$60,667	$1,183,000

Here is the analysis of the example using numbers.

On 4/10/2020, the three-year floating bond is issued. The spot LIBOR rate of 3.80 percent on 4/10/2020 determines the floating-rate coupon interest income on the next coupon-paying day, 10/10/2020. There are 183 days between 4/10/2020 and 10/10/2020 and the interest due is based on LIBOR plus 50 basis points.

$$\text{Interest due on October } 10, 2020 = 60,000,000 \times (0.038 + 0.005) \times \frac{183}{360}$$
$$= \$1,311,500$$

On 10/10/2020, the spot LIBOR rate turns out to be 4.90 percent.

$$\text{Interest due on April } 10, 2021 = 60,000,000 \times (0.049 + 0.005) \times \frac{182}{360}$$
$$= \$1,638,000$$

The first caplet and the first floorlet expire on 10/10/2020.

$$\text{First caplet payoff} = 60,000,000 \times max(4.90\% - 4.50\%, 0) \times \frac{182}{360}$$
$$= \$121,333$$
$$\text{First floorlet payoff} = 60,000,000 \times max(3.40\% - 4.90\%, 0) \times \frac{182}{360}$$
$$= \$0$$

The payoffs of the caplet and floorlet are paid on 4/10/2021. As a result, the effective interest payment is $1,311,500 on 10/10/2020.

On 04/10/2021, effective interest payment is:

$$\text{Effective interest payment on April 10, 2021} = 1,638,000 - 121,333 + 0$$
$$= \$1,516,667$$

On 04/10/2021, the spot LIBOR rate turns out to be 4.60 percent.

$$\text{Interest due on October 10, 2021} = 60,000,000 \times (0.046 + 0.005) \times \frac{183}{360}$$
$$= \$1,555,500$$

The second floorlet expires 04/10/2021.

$$\text{Second caplet payoff} = 60,000,000 \times \max(4.60\% - 4.50\%, 0) \times \frac{183}{360} = \$30,500$$

$$\text{Second floorlet payoff} = 60,000,000 \times \max(3.40\% - 4.60\%, 0) \times \frac{183}{360} = \$0$$

On 10/10/2021, effective interest payment is:

$$\text{Effective interest due on October 10, 2021} = 1,555,500 - 30,500 + 0$$
$$= \$1,525,000$$

The procedure is repeated at each coupon-paying day until the bond matures. The preceding table summarizes all transactions.

LESSON 3: OPTION PORTFOLIO RISK MANAGEMENT STRATEGIES

Option portfolio risk management: understand strategies related to hedging with options; interpret option delta, option gamma, and option vega.

LOS 33e: Explain why and how a dealer delta hedges an option position, why delta changes, and how the dealer adjusts to maintain the delta hedge. Vol 5, pp 333–343

LOS 33f: Interpret the gamma of a delta-hedged portfolio and explain how gamma changes as in-the-money and out-of-the-money options move toward expiration. Vol 5, pp 333–343

Risk Management of an Option Portfolio

So far, the hedging strategies using options have been discussed from an end-user's perspective. However, in every transaction, there is always a counter party. In most cases, the counter party of the end-user is an option market maker or option dealer. Option dealers make a market in options by providing liquidity and taking the opposite of the transaction. They generally charge a commission and they profit from the bid-ask spreads in option prices. However, option dealers often find that after they acquire an option position from an end-user, it is difficult to unload the exact option position to a different end-user. Consequently, option dealers need to manage the risk associated with their portfolio of options. In this section, strategies related to risk management of an option portfolio are examined.

Consider an option dealer who holds a position in an option portfolio. Options in the portfolio can be either long or short, call or put. For simplicity, assume the portfolio has only one long call position. To hedge the risk associated with this option, the option dealer may take any one of the following actions:

1. Sell an identical option;
2. Sell a synthetic option;
3. Use a fractional share of the underlying asset to hedge the option; or
4. Use another option to hedge the option.

Each one of the preceding strategies is described in greater detail:

1. *Sell an identical option*: The option dealer holds a long position in the option. If he sells the option, or sells an identical option, he is fully hedged. Everything sounds perfectly right. The only trouble is that it is hard to find a counterparty who wants to buy the option. Often, the options are tailored to specific needs of a client. It's difficult to find a counterparty to be interested in the option. This method does not work well in reality.
2. *Sell a synthetic option*: One way to create a synthetic option is to use the option put-call parity relation. Given the option dealer holds a long call option position, he can sell a synthetic call option to hedge. Option put-call parity relation suggests $c = S + p - PV(X)$. The portfolio on the right side of the equation is the synthetic call. To sell the synthetic call, the option dealer should sell a share of the underlying stock, sell an otherwise identical put option on the stock, and buy a risk free bond with the face value being the same as the exercise price of the call option. The above set of transactions makes perfect sense in theory. In reality, it is difficult to implement. Again, there may not be a put option that exactly corresponds to the call option. Even if there is such a put, the market for the put option may not be liquid and it may be difficult to find a counterparty who is willing to buy the put option from the option dealer. This method does not work well in reality.
3. *Use underlying stock to hedge the option*: In many cases, the best way to hedge an option position is to use the underlying asset. This concept is widely used in hedging; it is called option delta.

$$\text{Option delta} = \frac{\text{Change in option price}}{\text{Change in the underlying stock price}} = \frac{\Delta c}{\Delta S}$$

Consider an option dealer who holds some number of shares of a stock (Ns) and some number of call options (N_c) on the stock. Her portfolio value is given below:

$$V = N_S S + N_c c$$

Change in the portfolio value is:

$$\Delta V = N_S \Delta S + N_c \Delta c$$

The hedging goal is to make the portfolio to be insensitive to pricing changes (given a change in S, the change in $V = 0$). Dividing by ΔS:

$$\frac{\Delta V}{\Delta S} = N_S \frac{\Delta S}{\Delta S} + N_c \frac{\Delta c}{\Delta S}$$
$$= N_S + N_c \frac{\Delta c}{\Delta S}$$

Solving for N_c / N_S and setting the equation to zero:

$$\frac{N_c}{N_S} = -\frac{1}{\dfrac{\Delta c}{\Delta S}}$$

The above equation specifies that the ratio of calls to shares is equal to the negative of 1 over the delta. Note that the term $\dfrac{\Delta c}{\Delta S}$ is the option delta.

4. *Use another option to hedge the option*: The option dealer may hold other options on the same underlying asset. Other options with the same underlying stock may either increase or decrease the risk exposure of the existing option. Using the same logic above, assume there is a second option:

$$V = N_{c1} c_1 + N_{c2} c_2$$

Change in the portfolio value is:

$$\Delta V = N_{c1} \Delta c_1 + N_{c2} \Delta c_2$$

The hedging goal is to make the portfolio to be insensitive to pricing changes. Dividing by ΔS solving for N_1/N_2 and setting the equation to zero:

$$\frac{\Delta V}{\Delta S} = N_{c1} \frac{\Delta c_1}{\Delta S} + N c_2 \frac{\Delta c_2}{\Delta S}$$

$$\frac{N_1}{N_2} = -\frac{\Delta c_2}{\Delta c_1}$$

The above equation specifies the ratio of shares of another option needed to hedge a certain number of existing options. The negative sign indicates one position is long and the other is short.

In the above discussion, a static approach is taken and it is assumed that once a hedge is constructed, the hedged portfolio stays hedged during the remaining life of the option(s). However, in reality, it is not the case. Option delta changes as other factors that affect option prices change. For example, option delta changes when the underlying stock price changes and when the time to maturity of the option changes. The rate at which delta changes as the underlying stock price changes is called option gamma.

$$\text{Option gamma} = \frac{\text{Change in option delta}}{\text{Change in the underlying stock price}}$$

The fact that an option delta is not constant (option gamma is not zero) brings challenges in hedging. A delta-hedged position at current time may not be delta hedged any more after some time has elapsed because the new delta is no longer the same as the previous delta. The following application example examines the issue.

Example 3-1

A stock is traded at $100 per share. The stock does not pay any dividends. The annualized stock return standard deviation is 40 percent. A call option on the stock has an exercise price of $95 and a time to maturity of 3 months. Risk free rate is 5 percent per year. Assuming the Black-Scholes model, the option delta is 0.66.

A. How many shares are needed to hedge 2 call contracts?

B. How many call options are needed to hedge 400 shares?

The stock price changes to $97 and the option delta is 0.61.

C. How many shares are needed to hedge 2 call contracts?

D. How many call options are needed to hedge 400 shares?

E. What is the option gamma?

Solutions:

A. Every 0.66 shares hedge a short call option. There are 200 call options. You need to short $200 \times 0.66 = 132$ shares. To hedge 2 call option contracts, we need to sell 132 shares of the underlying stock.

B. Every 0.66 shares hedge a short call option. There are 400 shares. You need to short $400 \div 0.66 = 606$ call options. To hedge 400 shares, we need to sell 606 call options.

C. Every 0.61 shares hedge a short call option. There are 200 call options. You need to short $200 \times 0.61 = 122$ shares. To hedge 2 call option contracts, we need to sell 122 shares of the underlying stock.

D. Every 0.61 shares hedge a short call option. There are 400 shares. You need to short $400 \div 0.61 = 656$ call options. To hedge 400 shares, we need to sell 656 call options.

E. Option gamma:

$$\text{Option gamma} = \frac{0.61 - 0.66}{97 - 100} = 0.017$$

Volatility plays a significant role in option pricing. Option prices are particularly sensitive to volatility changes. The sensitivity of option price change with respect to stock return volatility change is called option vega. It is given by the following expression:

$$\text{Option vega} = \frac{\text{Change in option price}}{\text{Change in annualized stock return volatility}}$$

In summary, an option hedged position requires rebalancing to stay hedged because option delta changes when stock price, time to maturity, or stock return volatility changes. Rebalancing portfolios can be challenging and expensive. CFA candidates should understand risk factors associated with hedging. Specifically, candidates should be familiar with option delta, option gamma, and option vega.

READING 34: RISK MANAGEMENT APPLICATIONS OF SWAP STRATEGIES

Time to complete: 12 hours

Reading summary: This reading focuses on applications of swap strategies. Specifically, we examine how to use interest rate swaps, currency swaps, equity swaps, and swaptions. Interest rate swaps are used to achieve the following goals: (1) convert a floating rate bond to a fixed rate bond and vice versa; and (2) change the duration of a bond portfolio; Currency swaps are used to (1) convert a sequence of cash flows in foreign currency into cash flows in home currency; and (2) convert a domestic debt obligation into a foreign debt obligation and vice versa. Equity swaps are used to (1) diversify a concentrated equity portfolio; and (2) alter allocation weights in a stock-bond portfolio. Finally, interest rate swaptions are used to (1) change payment patterns of a sequence of future cash flows; and (2) terminate an existing swap.

We focus on derivative applications using swap contracts and swaptions in this reading. We consider three kinds of swaps: interest rate swaps, currency swaps, and equity swaps. Most of this reading is related to interest rate swaps. At the end of this reading, we have a section on interest rate swaptions and their applications.

LESSON 1: STRATEGIES AND APPLICATIONS FOR MANAGING INTEREST RATE RISK

Candidates should master the following hedging and speculation strategies:

Understand how to use *interest rate swaps* to:

- Synthetically convert a floating-rate bond to a fixed-rate bond, and vice versa.
- Adjust the duration of a fixed income portfolio.
- Create structured notes, including leveraged floating rate notes and inverse floaters.

INTEREST RATE SWAPS

An interest rate swap is a contractual agreement where the two counterparties agree to exchange cash flows over the life of the swap (tenor) based on a pair of coupon rates and a reference amount (notional principal). For example, a plain vanilla interest rate swap has one counterparty paying a fixed coupon rate and the other counterparty paying a floating rate. At initiation, none of the notional principal is exchanged because it simply serves as a reference amount from which to compute the periodic payments. On each of the payment dates, the fixed rate is unchanged but the floating rate fluctuates. If the floating rate rises above the fixed rate, the floating-rate payer makes a net payment to the fixed-rate payer. If the floating rate falls below the fixed rate, it is the fixed-rate payer that makes a net payment to the floating-rate payer.

To refresh you on a few of the technical details, at initiation the:

- Notional principal is *not* exchanged;
- Value of the contract is *zero*;
- *Price* of the contract is the fixed rate; and
- *Long* position is the fixed-rate payer.

The terminology used to describe swaps includes:

- *Counterparty* = the opposite side or position on the contract;
- *Notional* = reference amount on which periodic payments are based;

- *Tenor* = the duration or maturity of the swap;
- *Frequency* = how often payments are exchanged (monthly, quarterly, annually);
- *Fixed payment* = the static leg of the swap;
- *Floating payment* = the variable leg of the swap, usually based on LIBOR; and
- *Netting* = the practice by which the payments offset with the difference paid to only one party.

Exhibit 1-1: Plain Vanilla Interest Rate Swap

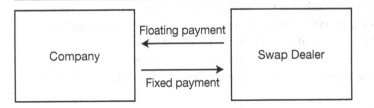

One quirk to remember is that floating payments are made in arrears, meaning that the variable rate today ($LIBOR_0$,) determines the *next* payment (PMT_1). In other words, we always know what the *next* payment will be.

Interest rate swaps are the most widely utilized instrument for managing interest rate risk. Recall that interest rate risk is a concern to borrowers, who could face rising interest expense, and lenders, who face declining portfolio value in response to changes in the level of interest rates.

Borrowers usually use swaps to alter the terms of their existing debt. The swap contract is an overlay position that exists concurrently with the original liability but offsets the cash flows to produce a desired net behavior of the combined position.

Lenders use swaps to alter the duration of their asset portfolio. By adding swaps to the portfolio, the investor may lengthen or shorten its duration in anticipation of falling or rising interest rates, thus increasing or decreasing the portfolio's sensitivity to interest rates.

A third application of swaps involves structured notes, which are synthetically designed instruments that have characteristics distinct from traditional fixed-income assets. Swaps are used to manage the interest rate risk associated with these customized securities.

LOS 34a: Demonstrate how an interest rate swap can be used to convert a floating-rate (fixed-rate) loan to a fixed-rate (floating-rate) loan.
Vol 5, pp 359–363

Convert a Floating Rate to a Fixed Rate

When seeking financing, many companies find it difficult to find a bank willing to lend funds at attractive fixed rates. Already facing credit risk, the bank often shifts the interest rate risk to the borrower. But, having secured financing at variable rates, the borrower now faces the risk of interest rates rising and interest expense increasing. To manage this risk, a swap contract can be used to effectively convert the loan from a variable rate to a fixed rate.

The key insight to an interest rate swap is that it can be viewed as a portfolio of a long position in a floating-rate bond and a short position in a fixed-rate bond. Stated another way, a *pay-fixed* position in a plain vanilla interest rate swap represents borrowing at a fixed rate and investing in a floating-rate bond. The swap is used to offset the position that you want to get rid of (floating-rate payments) and replace it with the exposure you do want (fixed-rate payments). Many difficult problems involving an interest rate swap can be solved easily when we apply this insight:

> [Pay fixed and receive floating interest rate swap] = Floating rate bond − Fixed rate bond

Conversion between a floating-rate bond and a fixed-rate bond can be algebraically achieved by simply rearranging the above equation.

A long position in a floating-rate bond can be achieved by using a long position in a fixed-rate bond and a pay-fixed receive-floating interest rate swap. This relation is useful when a portfolio manager who is holding a fixed-rate bond intends to convert it into a floating-rate bond, potentially due to expectations of an *increase* in interest rates.

> Floating rate bond = Fixed rate bond + [Pay fixed and receive floating interest rate swap]

A short position in a floating-rate bond can be achieved by using a short position in a fixed-rate bond and a short pay-fixed receive-floating interest rate swap (or a long pay floating and receive fixed interest rate swap). This relation is useful when a corporate manager who has issued a fixed-rate bond intends to convert it into a floating-rate bond, potentially due to expectations of a *decrease* in interest rates.

> −Floating rate bond = −Fixed rate bond − [Pay fixed and receive floating interest rate swap]

A long position in a fixed-rate bond can be achieved by using a long position in a floating-rate bond and a short pay-fixed receive-floating interest rate swap (or a long pay floating and receive fixed interest rate swap). This relation is useful when a portfolio manager who is holding a floating-rate bond intends to convert it into a fixed-rate bond, potentially due to expectations of a *decrease* in interest rates.

> Fixed rate bond = Floating rate bond − [Pay fixed and receive floating interest rate swap]

A short position in a fixed-rate bond can be achieved by using a short position in a floating-rate bond and a pay-fixed receive-floating interest rate swap. This relation is useful when a corporate manager who has issued a floating-rate bond intends to convert it into a fixed-rate bond, potentially due to expectations of an *increase* in interest rates.

> −Fixed rate bond = −Floating rate bond + [Pay fixed and receive floating interest rate swap]

Candidates should not attempt to memorize all equations for the previous four scenarios. Instead, fully understand the first equation, which states that an interest rate swap is a portfolio of two bonds. All remaining equations are simply transformations of the first equation.

We use an example to demonstrate how to convert a fixed-rate loan into a floating-rate loan.

Suppose a company went to a bank looking for fixed-rate financing. The bank declined to lend at an attractive fixed rate but offered to lend $5 million at a variable rate of LIBOR + 4 percent instead. How might the company use a plain vanilla interest rate swap to convert the variable-rate loan into a fixed-rate loan? Exhibit 1-2 illustrates how this might be accomplished with a swap having an 8 percent fixed rate and LIBOR flat as the variable rate.

Exhibit 1-2: Convert Floating-Rate Debt into Fixed-Rate Debt

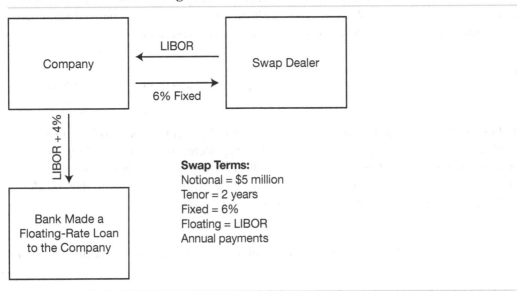

The company must still make floating payments to the bank based on the variable rate (LIBOR + 4%). The company should enter the swap as the fixed-rate payer (variable-rate receiver) to offset the outflow of variable interest payments to the bank. This is then replaced with the payment on the swap at the fixed rate. The net interest rate payable by the company is now:

$$\text{Net payment} = (\text{LIBOR} + 4\%) - \text{LIBOR} + 6\% = 10\%$$

Example 1-1

A corporation has an outstanding fixed-rate bond that was issued two years ago. At issue, the bond has a five-year to maturity. The fixed coupon rate is 8 percent. Coupon payments are due semiannually. Today the bond has three years to maturity. Managers in the corporation believe that interest rates will likely decrease significantly over the next three-year period and would like to convert the debt into a floating-rate bond.

A. **Describe** a strategy to achieve management's goal using an interest rate swap.

   The outstanding face value of the bond issue is $50 million. The firm negotiates an interest rate swap where the firm pays six-month LIBOR rate and receives 5.4 percent. Cash settlements are semiannual based on a day count of #days/360. Settlement dates match coupon paying dates of the firm's bonds. The notional matches the size of the bond issue. The current six-month LIBOR rate is 6.1 percent.

B. **Calculate** the next net cash flow considering both the loan and the swap.

Solutions:

A. The firm wants to offset its fixed-rate bond and be left with a floating-rate payment. To convert the fixed-rate bond into a floating-rate bond, the firm should enter a pay-floating / receive-fixed interest rate swap.

   −Floating rate bond = −Fixed rate bond −[Pay fixed and receive floating interest rate swap]

B. The firm's cash flows have two components:
   Cash flow directly to firm's bondholders:

   $$\text{Cash outflow} = 50 \times \frac{0.08}{2} = \$2 \, \text{million per six months}$$

   Cash flows from the interest rate swap:

   $$\text{Cash inflow} = 50 \times 0.054 \times \frac{\#\text{days}}{360} = \text{per six months}$$

   $$\text{Cash outflow} = 50 \times \text{LIBOR} \times \frac{\#\text{days}}{360} = \text{per six months}$$

   Overall, the firm pays: LIBOR + 8% − 5.4% = LIBOR + 2.6%, which is a floating rate.

   $$\text{Net outflow} = \left(\frac{\text{LIBOR} + 2.6\%}{2} \right) \$50 \, \text{million}$$

   $$= \left(\frac{0.0877}{2} \right) \$50 \, \text{million} = \$2.19 \, \text{million}$$

We use another example to demonstrate how to convert a floating-rate loan into a fixed-rate loan.

Example 1-2

An investment firm holds $10 million face value of a floating-rate bond issued by a local firm. The floating rate is based on six-month LIBOR with a credit spread of 300 basis points. Cash settlements are semiannual. Day count is #days/360. The bond has four years remaining to maturity. Managers of the firm predict that short-term interest rates are likely to decrease significantly over the next four years and would like to lock in a fixed rate using an interest rate swap.

    A. **Describe** the strategy the firm should take using a plain vanilla interest rate swap.

        Assume that the firm negotiates an interest rate swap where the firm pays six-month LIBOR rate and receives 5.3 percent. Settlement dates match coupon paying dates of the firm's bonds. Swap notional principal is $10 million, matching the size of the floating-rate bond holding. The current six-month LIBOR rate is 5.8 percent.

    B. **Calculate** the net interest rate the firm should receive on the combined position.

Solutions:

    A. The investment firm holds a long position in a floating-rate bond. The bond has four years to maturity. To convert the floating-rate bond into a fixed-rate bond, the investment firm should enter a pay floating and receive fixed interest rate swap.

$$\text{Fixed-rate bond} = \text{Floating-rate bond} + [\text{Pay floating and receive fixed interest rate swap}]$$

    B. The investment firm's cash flows have two components: Cash flow directly from floating-rate bonds:

$$\text{Cash inflow} = 10 \times (\text{LIBOR} + 3\%) \times \frac{\#\text{days}}{360} = \text{per six months}$$

Cash flows from the interest rate swap:

$$\text{Cash inflow} = 50 \times 0.053 \times \frac{\#\text{days}}{360} = \text{per six months}$$

$$\text{Cash outflow} = 10 \times \text{LIBOR} \times \frac{\#\text{days}}{360} = \text{per six months}$$

Overall, the investment firm collects: $(\text{LIBOR} + 3\%) + 5.3\% - \text{LIBOR} = 8.3\%$, which is a fixed rate.

LOS 34b: Calculate and interpret the duration of an interest rate swap. Vol 5, pp 363–366

Change the Duration of a Fixed-Income Portfolio

An important part of risk management for a fixed income portfolio is managing interest rate risk, which is the uncertainty of the value of the portfolio due to changes in the underlying yields. A commonly used measure of interest rate risk is duration. Bond duration is important for risk management because it directly measures the dollar exposure of a fixed income portfolio when the underling yield changes.

Active bond portfolio managers often dynamically alter the duration of their bond portfolios to reflect their tactical predictions of interest rate movements. An active bond fund manager may choose to increase the portfolio's duration when the he predicts falling interest rates and shorten the duration if he expects interest rates to rise. However, bond markets tend to be relatively illiquid. Therefore, trading bonds generally involves high transaction costs. Instead, managers often rely on derivative contracts to achieve hedging or speculative positions without incurring the added costs of trading actual bonds in and out of the portfolio. In this section, we investigate how to use interest rate swaps to adjust the duration of a bond portfolio.

The key insight is again very simple. A plain vanilla interest rate swap can be viewed as a long position in a floating-rate bond and a short position in a fixed-rate bond. Consequently, the duration of an interest rate swap is the difference in duration of the two positions.

[Pay fixed and receive floating interest rate swap] = Floating rate bond – Fixed rate bond

Recall that the duration of a fixed-rate bond is heavily influenced by its maturity. In fact, the duration of a fixed-rate bond can be estimated to be approximately 75 percent of the time to its maturity. The duration of a floating-rate bond is much shorter and can be estimated to be about one-half of its coupon reset period. For example, duration of a 10-year fixed-rate bond is approximately 75 percent of 10 years, which is 7.5. Duration of a 5-year floating-rate bond with semiannual payments is approximately 50 percent of six months (coupon reset period), which is 25.

In practice, a bond's duration is also affected by the size of the coupon, the frequency of payment, and the level of interest rates. We use these approximations for convenience and expediency.

LOS 34c: Explain the effect of an interest rate swap on an entity's cash flow risk. Vol 5, pp 366–370

Let's look at a few examples of duration of interest rate swaps.

Decrease Portfolio Duration

Swap A: Pay 6 percent fixed and receive 180-day LIBOR. Payments are reset semiannually. The swap tenor is five years. This swap can be viewed as a long floating-rate bond based on 180-day LIBOR and a short 6 percent fixed-rate bond. Both bonds have a maturity of five years. The fixed-rate bond has an approximate duration of 75 percent of five years, or 3.75. The floating-rate bond has an approximate duration of 50 percent of 0.5 years (based on semiannual coupon resets), or 0.25. Because we're taking the fixed-rate payer side, the fixed-rate bond is in the short position, and the floating-rate bond is in the long position, the interest rate swap's net duration is:

$$
\begin{array}{c}
\text{Duration of [Pay fixed and receive} \\
\text{floating interest rate swap]}
\end{array}
=
\begin{array}{c}
\text{Duration of} \\
\text{(floating-rate bond)}
\end{array}
-
\begin{array}{c}
\text{Duration of} \\
\text{(fixed-rate bond)}
\end{array}
$$

$$= 0.25 - 3.75 = -3.50$$

Note that the duration of the swap is negative because the long floating-rate bond has a smaller duration (of 0.25) than the short fixed-rate bond (which has a duration of 3.75). The interest rate swap has a duration of *negative* 3.5. When this swap is added to a fixed income portfolio, the net duration of the portfolio *decreases*.

Increase Portfolio Duration

Swap B: Receive 8 percent fixed and pay 90-day LIBOR. Payments are reset quarterly. Swap tenor is four years. This swap can be viewed as a short floating-rate bond based on 90-day LIBOR and a long 8 percent fixed-rate bond. Both bonds have a maturity of four years. The fixed-rate bond has an approximate duration of 75 percent of four years, or 3.0. The floating-rate bond has an approximate duration of 50 percent of 0.25 years (based on quarterly coupon resets), or 0.125. Because the fixed-rate bond is in a long position and the floating-rate bond is in a short position, the interest rate swap has a net duration of:

$$
\begin{array}{c}
\text{Duration of [Pay floating and receive} \\
\text{fixed interest rate swap]}
\end{array}
=
\begin{array}{c}
\text{Duration of} \\
\text{(fixed-rate bond)}
\end{array}
-
\begin{array}{c}
\text{Duration of} \\
\text{(floating-rate bond)}
\end{array}
$$

$$= 3.0 - 0.125 = 2.875$$

Note that the duration of the swap is positive because the long fixed-rate bond has a larger duration (of 3.0) than the short floating-rate bond (which has a duration of 0.125). The interest rate swap has a duration of *positive* 2.875. When this swap is added to a fixed income portfolio, the duration of the portfolio *increases*.

Achieve a Target Portfolio Duration

Now that we've calculated the duration of a swap and determined which side of the swap we should take in order to increase or decrease the duration of our portfolio, the final piece of the puzzle is choosing the notional amount that, when the swap is combined with our existing portfolio, produces the net duration that we want to achieve. To accomplish this, we want to match the dollar duration of the portfolio + swap position with the target dollar duration. Recall that dollar duration is simply the duration times the value, and for a swap it's the duration times the notional.

$$\$DUR_{(P+S)} = \$DUR_{\text{Target}}$$
$$V_P(DUR_P) + NP(DUR_S) = V_P(DUR_T)$$

For example, a portfolio manager has a bond fund with $400 million and a modified duration of 5.80 as of today. She expects interest rates to rise over the next 12 to 18 months and wants to lower the fund's duration to 5.10 for the next two years. She decides to enter a two-year plain vanilla interest rate swap with a 5 percent fixed leg and a floating leg of LIBOR + 2 percent. The swap has annual settlement dates.

LOS 34d: Determine the notional principal value needed on an interest rate swap to achieve a desired level of duration in a fixed-income portfolio. Vol 5, pp 363–366

We want to match the dollar duration of the portfolio and swap position combination to the target dollar duration.

$$V_P(DUR_P) + NP(DUR_S) = V_P(DUR_T)$$
$$\$400(5.8) + NP(DUR_S) = \$400(5.10)$$

Since we want to *lower* the portfolio's duration, we take the pay-fixed (receive-floating) side of the swap and estimate the swap's duration to be:

$$DUR_S = DUR_{\text{Float}} - DUR_{\text{Fixed}} = 0.5 - 1.5 = -1.0$$

Plugging this into our equation and solving for the notional principal (*NP*), we get:

$$\$400(5.8) + NP(-1.0) = \$400(5.10)$$
$$NP = V_p\left(\frac{DUR_T - DUR_P}{DUR_S}\right) = \$280\,\text{million}$$

Example 1-3

A bond fund manager holds $60 million of bonds with a duration of 7.80. The manager would like to increase the duration of the bond fund to 8.80 by using interest rate swaps. The manager has the following swap available to her:

Five-year, pay-fixed 6 percent and receive-floating 180-day LIBOR with semiannual payments.

- A. **Determine** whether she should buy or sell the swap.

- B. To achieve the target duration of 8.80, **calculate** the notional principal that should be set on the interest rate swap.

Solutions:

- A. The interest rate swap has the following duration:

  $$0.5 \times 0.5 - 0.75 \times 5 = -3.50$$

  Note that the fund manager intends to *increase* the duration of her bond portfolio. She should *sell* the swap, meaning that she should *pay floating rate* of 180-day LIBOR and *receive fixed* rate of 6 percent. The duration of the short swap is positive 3.50.

- B. The target duration is the weighted average duration of the existing bond duration and swap duration:

  $$60 \times 7.8 + NP \times 3.5 = 60 \times 8.8$$
  $$NP = \$17.1429 \, \text{million}$$

Creating Structured Notes

Structured notes are floating-rate instruments with some sort of embedded exotic feature. One feature could be leverage, where the floating rate is a multiple of a benchmark rate, such as LIBOR. Another feature might be to have the coupon rate move inversely to a benchmark rate. Features can also be combined to make a leveraged inverse floater.

These securities are sold to institutions, like insurance companies, that might want custom features or are precluded from investing using derivatives or margin. Structured notes are considered fixed-income securities under most regulatory regimes, allowing the buyer to "get around" regulator barriers. The designers of these instruments issue the note with the features spelled out and then replicate their characteristics using derivatives, usually earning a spread of the price of the note and the derivative positions used to offset it.

In this section, we examine two kinds of structured securities, leveraged structured notes and inverse floating rate notes. We use the following notations in our discussions.

F_N: the face value of the structured note.
F_B: the face value or principal of a bond.
NP: the notional principal of the swap.
c_B: the coupon rate of a fixed-rate bond.
r_S: the fixed rate of an interest rate swap.

Note that, by definition, r_S is the fixed rate that makes the value of the interest rate swap equal to *zero* at swap initiation.

Leveraged Floating-Rate Notes

Now, we use an example to examine the structure of a leveraged floating-rate structured note. Consider the following case.

a. Investment Bank X (IBX) sells a leveraged floating-rate note to Hedge Fund Y (HFY). The leveraged floating-rate note pays annual coupons based on 2.5 times the 180-day LIBOR rate. The face value of the note (F_N) is $40 million. The time to maturity is six years.

b. To offset the payments it must make to HFY, IBX enters a swap with Dealer Z. Under the terms of the swap agreement, IBX pays a fixed rate of r_S and receives a floating rate of 180-day LIBOR. Swap payments are made annually. The notional principal (NP) is $100 million (2.5 times F_N). The time to maturity is six years to match the structured note.

c. Finally, to cover the fixed payments owed on the swap, IBX buys a fixed-rate bond issued by Corporation A. The fixed-coupon rate is c_B. Coupon payments are made annually. The face value of the bond position is $100 million (2.5 times F_N). The time to maturity matches both the structured note and the swap.

The deal is diagramed in Exhibit 1-3.

Exhibit 1-3: Leveraged Floater Deal between IBX and HFY

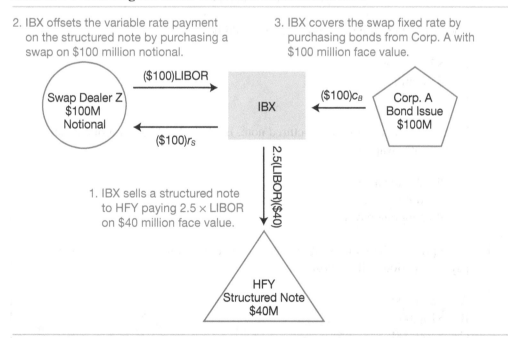

2. IBX offsets the variable rate payment on the structured note by purchasing a swap on $100 million notional.

3. IBX covers the swap fixed rate by purchasing bonds from Corp. A with $100 million face value.

1. IBX sells a structured note to HFY paying 2.5 × LIBOR on $40 million face value.

Let's analyze IBX's cash inflows and outflows:

Cash inflows
1. Fixed coupon income from Corp. A: $100 million × LIBOR
2. Floating-rate payment from interest rate swap: $100 million × LIBOR

Cash outflows
1. Floating-rate coupon payment to HFY: $40 million × 2.5 × LIBOR
2. Fixed-rate payment from swap: $100 million × r_S

The net cash flow for IBX is:

$$NCF_{IBX} = (\$100M)c_B + (\$100M)\text{LIBOR} - (2.5)(\$40M)\text{LIBOR} - (\$100M)r_S$$
$$= (\$100M)(c_b - r_s)$$

To summarize, a leveraged floating rate note with face value of F_N and a leverage factor of k can be synthetically created by combining a fixed-rate bond with a face value of $k \times F_N$ and a fixed coupon rate of c_B with an interest rate swap having a notional principal of $k \times F_N$ and a fixed rate of r_S. Note that the portfolio of a fixed-rate bond and an interest rate swap does not *exactly* replicate the leveraged floating rate note. There is a difference of $(k \times F_N)(c_B - r_S)$ in annual payments. If structured correctly, that difference represents a net cash *inflow* to IBX.

Example 1-4

Bank A holds $60 million face value of a five-year fixed-rate bond that pays 4.5 percent coupon on a semiannual basis. Bank A wishes to sell a leveraged floating-rate note against the fixed-rate bond holdings. The leveraged floating rate is based on 1.2 times 180-day LIBOR rate. Coupon payments are semiannual.

1. The face value of the structured note should be *closest* to:

    A. $50 million.
    B. $60 million.
    C. $72 million.

2. To manage the risk of the structured note, Bank A should enter a plain vanilla interest rate swap as the:

    A. fixed-rate payer.
    B. fixed-rate receiver.
    C. floating rate payer.

3. If the price of the swap is 4.0 percent, the net cash flow at the end of each payment period will be *closest* to:

    A. −$250,000
    B. $150,000
    C. $300,000

Solutions:

1. A. The structured note pays a leveraged coupon. Therefore, the face value of the bond, F_B, and the notional of the swap used to cover the payments on the note must be the leverage factor, k, times the face value of the note, F_N. Solving for F_N:

$$F_B = k(F_N) = 1.2(F_N) = \$60 \text{ million}$$

$$F_N = \frac{\$60M}{1.20} = \$50 \text{ million}$$

2. A. The swap is used to offset the leveraged floating-rate payment on the structured note. Therefore, Bank A should receive the floating payment, taking the fixed-rate payer position on the swap.

3. B. The cash flows to Bank A can be summarized as follows:

+ Fixed-rate payment on bond =	$\$60(0.045/2)$
− Fixed-rate payment on swap =	$\$60(0.040/2)$
+ Floating-rate payment on swap =	$\$60(\text{LIBOR}/2)$
− Floating-rate payment on note =	$\$50(1.20)(\text{LIBOR}/2)$

$$NCF = kFN(cB - r_S) = \$60 \text{ million } (0.045/2 - 0.040/2) = \$150,000$$

Don't forget the payments are semiannual, so divide all rates by two.

Inverse Floating-Rate Notes

Next, we examine the structure of an inverse floater. An inverse floater is a floating rate note whose coupon rate is inversely related to a benchmark rate, such as LIBOR. In other words, when LIBOR rises, the coupon on the inverse floater falls, and vice versa. The general form of coupon rate of an inverse floater is given by the following expression:

$$\text{Coupon rate of an inverse floater} = \max(b - k \times \text{LIBOR}, 0), \text{where } b > 0 \text{ and } k > 0$$

In our discussion, we will not use a leverage factor, $k = 1.0$, but in reality, k does not have to be one. The coupon rate of an inverse floater cannot be negative. When the expression for coupon rate yields a negative number, the coupon rate is assumed to be zero.

Here, we again rely on an example to illustrate the structure of an inverse floater.

a. Institution Zeta (Inst. Z) makes market in inverse floaters. Its most recent deal involves selling an inverse floating-rate note to Pension Fund Alpha (PFA). The inverse floater has a face value of $100 million. The benchmark rate is 180-day LIBOR. Coupon rate of the inverse floater is (12% − LIBOR). Coupon payments are made annually. The current 180-day LIBOR is 4.2 percent. The time to maturity of the inverse floater is four years.

b. To manage the risk associated with uncertainty in LIBOR rates, Institution Zeta sells an interest rate swap. In the interest swap, Institution Zeta pays 180-day LIBOR rate and receives r_S fixed rate. The notional principal is $100 million and tenor is four years.

c. At the same time, Institution Zeta holds $100 million face value of 6.2 percent fixed-rate bonds issued by Corporation Beta. The time to maturity of the fixed-rate bond is four years.

Exhibit 1-4: Inverse Floater Deal between Inst. Z and PFA

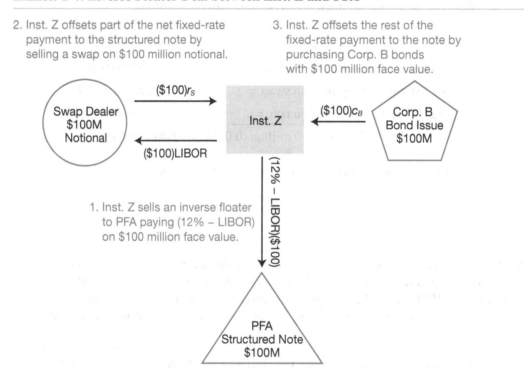

Let's analyze cash flows of Institution Zeta:

- Zeta pays inverse floater coupon interest to Alpha: $100 million × (12% − LIBOR)
- Zeta collects fixed rate coupon interest from Beta: $100 million × 6.2%
- Zeta pays floating rate in the interest rate swap: $100 million × LIBOR
- Zeta collect fixed rate in the interest rate swap: $100 million × r_S

Using annualized rates, the net cash flow to Zeta is:

$$
\begin{aligned}
NCF_{InstZ} &= r_S(kF_N) - \text{LIBOR}(kF_N) + c_B(kF_N) - k(b - \text{LIBOR})(F_N) \\
&= (r_S + c_B - b)(kF_N) \\
&= r_S(\$100) - \text{LIBOR}(\$100) + c_B(\$100) - b(\$100) + \text{LIBOR}(\$100) \\
&= r_S(\$100) + c_B(\$100) - b(\$100) \\
&= (r_S - 0.058)(\$100)
\end{aligned}
$$

There is another risk that Institution Zeta should address. If the LIBOR rate rises higher than b, in this case 13 percent, the inverse floater pays zero coupon interest, but the swap will still require a payment on the floating leg. As the LIBOR rate rises higher, the net cash flow to Zeta becomes increasingly negative. Buying an interest rate cap on LIBOR with a strike rate at b will hedge this risk. As LIBOR rises above b, the cap will be in-the-money, and any loss associated with LIBOR > b will be offset by the payoff on the cap.

To summarize, the payment on an inverse floater, $(b - \text{LIBOR})$, can be synthetically created using a portfolio consisting of a long position in a fixed-rate bond with a coupon rate of c_B and a short position (pay-floating/receive-fixed) in an interest rate swap with a fixed rate of r_S. Note, however, that the portfolio does not *exactly* replicate the inverse floater. There is a difference of $kF_N(r_S + c_B - b)$ at each payment date. If we combine the fixed difference in annual payment with the fixed-rate bond, we conclude that an inverse floater is a portfolio of a fixed-rate bond and an interest rate swap.

Example 1-5

An investment bank agreed to create a three-year, leveraged inverse floater with a face value of $20 million. The bank wants to earn a 25 basis point spread on each payment over the life of the deal. The coupon rate of the floater, which pays interest semiannually, is given by the following equation:

$$\text{Coupon rate} = 1.5[\max(10\% - \text{LIBOR}, 0)]$$

To manage the risk of this instrument, the investment bank buys a 6 percent, three-year corporate bond also paying interest semiannually. It also enters a plain vanilla swap contract with a dealer.

1. The appropriate notional principal on the swap required to offset the coupon rate of the structured note is *closest* to:

    A. $20 million.
    B. $30 million.
    C. $40 million.

2. If LIBOR is not expected to exceed 10% over the life of the note, the terms at which it should enter the swap are *closest* to a price of:

    A. 4.0 percent on a long position in the swap.
    B. 4.5 percent on a short position in the swap.
    C. 4.0 percent on a short position in the swap.

---

3. If the bank gets the swap terms it wants and LIBOR rises to 11%, the bank will *most likely* earn:

A. more than its 25 basis point spread.
B. its 25 basis point spread if it buys a cap with a 10 percent strike rate.
C. less than its 25 basis point spread unless it buys a cap with a strike rate above 11 percent.

Solutions:

1. B. This is a *leveraged* inverse floater, which will require the notional principal on the swap to be equal to the leverage factor times the face value of the structured note, $kF_N = 1.5(\$20 \text{ million}) = \$30 \text{ million}$.

2. B. Recall that the price of a swap is the fixed rate. The appropriate position in the swap is to pay floating and receive fixed. This is the short position in the swap. As long as LIBOR does not exceed 10%, b, the spread the bank can expect to earn will be:

$$\text{Spread} = r_S + c_B - b$$
$$0.25\% = \frac{r_S + 6.0\% - 10.0\%}{2}$$
$$r_S = 4.5\%$$

Remember that the structured note, the swap, and the bond all pay semiannual interest, requiring us to divide the annual rates by two.

3. B. If LIBOR rises above b, 10%, the bank will not pay on the structured note because its coupon cannot drop below zero. However, it will still have to pay the floating-rate leg of the swap. Assuming the bank got a price of 4.5 percent on the swap, the spread it earns on each payment date will be:

$$\text{Spread} = r_S + c_B - \text{LIBOR}$$
$$= \frac{4.5\% + 6.0\% - 11.0\%}{2} = -0.25\%$$

The bank can hedge this risk by purchasing a cap (call option on an interest rate) with a strike price of b, 10%. When LIBOR rises above 10%, the cap is in-the-money, offsetting the loss on LIBOR rising above b.

LESSON 2: STRATEGIES AND APPLICATIONS FOR MANAGING EXCHANGE RATE RISK

Candidates should master the following hedging and speculation strategies:

Understand how to use *currency swaps* to:

- Synthetically convert a bond denominated in one currency to a bond denominated in another currency.
- Convert foreign currency receipts into domestic currency using a currency swap that does not have initial or final exchange of notional principals.
- Manage currency risk and interest rate risk associated with a dual currency bond.

CURRENCY SWAPS

A currency swap is a contract where the counterparties agree to exchange cash flows that are denominated in different currencies. Like interest rate swaps, the size of the periodic payments are determined by an interest rate applied to the notional principal. These rates can be fixed and floating, like a plain vanilla interest rate swap, or any other combination (fixed-for-fixed, floating-for-floating).

Where currency swaps differ from interest rate swaps include:

- At initiation, the notionals are exchanged;
- The payments are *not* netted; and
- At expiration, the notionals are returned.

Exhibit 2-1 illustrates a fixed-for-fixed currency swap exchanging USD for EUR on $20 million with a spot exchange rate at initiation of USD 1.12 per EUR.

Exhibit 2-1: Fixed-for-Fixed Currency Swap USD/EUR

Initiation:
Exchange of notionals at USD 1.12 per EUR on USD 20 million

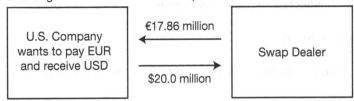

Payments:
Company receives fixed rate of 4.0% in USD and pays EUR at 3.4%

Expiration:
Return of notionals at USD 1.12 per EUR on USD 20 million

Firms might be motivated to enter a currency swap in order to change the currency denomination of debt, match foreign currency revenues with domestic currency expenses, or to manage the currency risk of foreign denominated assets.

LOS 34e: Explain how a company can generate savings by issuing a loan or bond in its own currency and using a currency swap to convert the obligation into another currency. Vol 5, pp 370–375

Change the Currency Denomination of Debt

The conversion of a bond denominated in one currency into a bond denominated in anther currency is a popular use of a currency swap. Consider the following example.

A U.S. firm wants to build a factory in Sydney, Australia. To finance the build, the firm needs to borrow AUD 40 million, which is USD 30.53 million at the currency exchange rate of AUD 1.310 per USD.

The firm is well established in the U.S. and can borrow locally for five years at 6 percent in USD. However, because the firm is not known in Australia, the firm's cost of debt is significantly higher there. The firm intends to borrow domestically in USD and use a currency swap to convert its debt to Australian dollars, which it can then use to finance the Australian project.

The firm and a swap dealer negotiate a currency swap with the following terms:

- Notional principals are AUD 40 million and USD 30.53.
- Tenor is 5 years.
- Fixed rate on the AUD payment is 2 percent and the fixed rate on the USD payment is 4 percent.
- Payments are semiannual. Payment dates match coupon payment dates of the firm's 6 percent USD debt.
- Notional principals are exchanged at both the initiation and expiration of the contract.

Initiating the Financing Deal ($t = 0$)

The firm's cash flows at inception are illustrated in Exhibit 2-2.

Exhibit 2-2: Initial Payments on Currency Swap

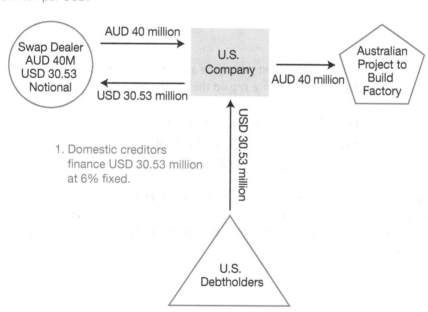

2. Swap contract exchanges notional at the current exchange rate of AUD1.31 per USD.

3. Company now has AUD to finance the factory in Australia.

AUD 40 million

Swap Dealer
AUD 40M
USD 30.53
Notional

U.S. Company

AUD 40 million

Australian Project to Build Factory

USD 30.53 million

USD 30.53 million

1. Domestic creditors finance USD 30.53 million at 6% fixed.

U.S. Debtholders

Making Periodic Payments: Semiannual Payments ($t = 1$ to 10)

At each payment date, the interest payments to the debtholders and the swap payments are aligned so that the cash flows are the following:

a. Cash outflow to USD bondholders   USD 0.916 million.
b. Cash inflow from currency swap   USD 0.611 million.
c. Cash outflow from currency swap   AUD 0.400 million.

Exhibit 2-3: Periodic Payments on Currency Swap

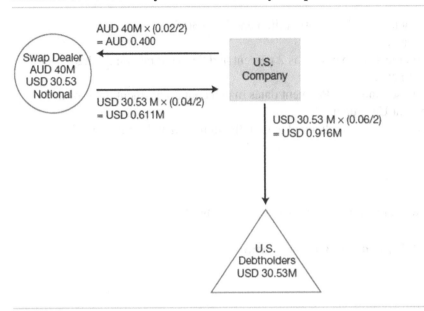

Swap at Expiration ($t = 10$)

After five years, the last swap and interest payments are made, the swap is unwound by the return of notionals, and the debtholders are repaid their principal.

a. Cash outflow to USD debtholders   USD 31.53 million.

b. Cash inflow from currency swap   USD 31.14 million.

c. Cash outflow from currency swap   AUD 40 million.

Notice that the same notional amounts are exchanged at the end as at initiation. At the spot exchange rate prevailing at $t = 0$, the net value of the exchange was zero. However, by the time the swap expires, the prevailing exchange rate has likely changed, and the net notional value will no longer be zero.

Example 2-1

Due to popular demand, a German auto manufacturer has recently built a production plant outside Shanghai, China. However, the German firm needs another CNY 900 million (Chinese currency) in working capital. Managers intend to issue a 5-year bond to raise funds for the firm's working capital. Interest rates in China are quite low to its domestic issuers. However, rates are much higher for foreign issuers. The firm is not interested in directly borrowing funds in the local Chinese debt market at high rates. Instead, the firm borrows euros in Germany at 4 percent for 5 years. Additionally, the firm enters a fixed-for-fixed currency swap. The interest rates on the currency swap are negotiated to be 4 percent on euro and 6 percent on CNY. The spot exchange rate is CNY 10 per EUR.

Here are the basic terms of the currency swap:

- Notional principals are ¥900 million (CNY) and €90 million (euros).
- Tenor is 5 years.
- Fixed rate on euros is 4 percent and fixed rate on CNY is 6 percent.
- Payments are semiannual. Payment dates match coupon payment dates of the firm's 4-percent bond in euros.
- Notional principals are exchanged at both the initiation and tenor of the swap.

Describe the cash flows of the currency swap and **demonstrate** that the swap converts a euro debt into a CNY debt.

Solution:

With the euro bond and the currency swap, the net cash flows of the German firm are listed below:

At time $t = 0$:

Cash inflow from euro bond issue	€90 million
Cash inflow from currency swap	¥900 million
Cash outflow from currency swap	€90 million
Net cash flow at time $t = 0$	cash inflow of ¥900 million

At time $t = 0.5, 1, 1.5, …, 4.5,$ and 5:

Cash outflow to euro bondholders	€90 × 0.04 = €3.6 million
Cash inflow from currency swap	€90 × 0.04 = €3.6 million
Cash outflow from currency swap	¥900 × 0.06 = ¥54 million
Net cash flow at time $t = 0.5, 1, …, 4.5, 5$	cash inflow of ¥54 million

At time $t = 5$:

Cash outflow from euro bondholders	€90 million
Cash inflow from currency swap	€90 million
Cash outflow from currency swap	¥900 million
Net cash flow at time $t = 5$	cash outflow of ¥900 million

Without the currency swap, the original debt is a standard fixed-rate bond denominated in euros. Combined with the currency swap, the net cash flows represent cash flows of a standard fixed-rate bond denominated in CNY. The currency swap has successfully converted a euro-denominated debt to a CNY denominated debt.

LOS 34f: Demonstrate how a firm can use a currency swap to convert a series of foreign cash receipts into domestic cash receipts. **Vol 5, pp 375–377**

Convert Foreign Cash Flows into Domestic Cash Flows

Some companies have foreign affiliates that generate consistent cash flows. When the firm wants to make regular cash transfers to the domestic headquarters, the funds can be protected against exchange rate movements with a currency swap that locks in the current exchange rate.

In a very simple way, let's consider the following situation. A U.S. retiree decides to spend the next five years in Quebec, Canada, learning French and enjoying fine dining. She does not intend to spend her savings, but instead plans to use her pension income to support her lifestyle in Canada. She collects an annuity of USD 200,000 per year, indefinitely. The spot exchange rate is CAD 1.06 per USD. How can she use a currency swap to hedge currency risk?

Suppose we negotiate with a swap dealer and structure a currency swap for her. The currency swap rates are based on the current term-structure of interest rates in U.S. and Canada. The U.S. dollar (USD) rate is 4.0 percent of USD notional principal and the Canadian dollar (CAD) rate is 3.8 percent of the CAD notional principal. So we have the following analysis of a currency swap to help the client who intends to spend the next five years in Canada:

- There is no exchange of notional principals in the currency swap.
- The tenor of currency swap is five years.
- Payments are annual, at the end of each year for five years.
- The client receives USD 200,000 per year from her pension. She would like to swap out USD cash flows and swap in CAD cash flows.

Her pension income of $200,000 should be 4.0 percent of the USD notional principal. We have:

$$\text{USD notional} \times 4.0\% = \text{USD}\,200,000$$

$$\text{USD notional} = \frac{\text{USD}\,200,000}{0.04} = \text{USD}\,5,000,000$$

Canadian dollar notional principal is based on the exchange rate of CAD 1.06 per USD. We have:

$$\text{USD notional} \times \frac{\text{CAD}\,1.06}{\text{USD}} = \text{CAD notional}$$

$$\text{CAD notional} = \text{USD}\,5,000,000 \times \text{CAD}\frac{1.06}{\text{USD}} = \text{CAD}\,5,300,000$$

The currency swap pays 3.8 percent of Canadian dollar notional principal:

$$CAD \text{ annual payment} = CAD\,5,300,000 \times 3.8\% = CAD\,201,400$$

Using this special currency swap, which does not involve exchanging notional principals at either the beginning or the end of the swap, the client has successfully converted an annual USD cash flow of 200,000 to an annual CAD cash flow of 201,400: The currency swap requires that she pays 4.0 percent of the U.S. dollar notional principal of $5 million, which is $200,000 per year, and that she receives 3.8 percent of the Canadian dollar notional principal of CAD 5.3 million, which is CAD 201,400.

To summarize, to convert an annuity of X units of funds in currency A into an annuity of Y units of funds in currency B, we should do the following.

Negotiate a currency swap between currency A and currency B. The currency swap should not involve exchange of notional principals at either the initiation or the end of the swap.

Let the fixed swap rate on currency A be *rate A* and let the fixed swap rate on currency B be *rate B*. The notional principal of currency A is given below:

$$NP(A) = \frac{X}{rate\ A}$$

Notional principal of currency B is given below:

$$NP(B) = \frac{NP(A)}{\text{Spot price of currency } B \text{ in currency } A}$$

Finally, the target Y units of funds in currency B that the annuity of X units of funds in currency A can be converted into is given below:

$$Y = NP(B) \times rate\ B$$

The previous example follows exactly the steps to reach the final answer. We use the following exercise to further demonstrate the procedure.

Example 2-2

A French Company X expects to have an annual $10 million after-tax income from its operations in the U.S. The cash flow is expected to last seven years. Company X intends to convert the income in U.S. dollars into its home currency, euros. The firm negotiates a currency swap that does not involve exchanging of notional principals. The fixed-for-fixed currency swap specifies a 4 percent rate on USD and 3.8 percent rate on EUR. The spot exchange rate is USD 1.38 per EUR. Compute the amount of notional principals in the currency swap and compute the amount of UER Company X is able to receive using the currency swap.

Solution:

We closely follow the steps listed above:

Negotiate a currency swap between U.S. dollars and euros. No notional principal exchange. Tenor is seven years. Settlement is annual.

Notional principal in U.S. dollars should be:

$$NP(A) = \frac{X}{rate\ A} = \frac{10}{0.04} = \$250\ \text{million}$$

Notional principal in euros should be:

$$NP(B) = \frac{NP(A)}{\text{Spot price of currency } B \text{ in currency } A}$$

$$= \frac{250}{1.38} = €181.16\ \text{million}$$

Finally, the amount of annuity in euros is computed as:

$$Y = NP(B) \times rate\ B = 181.16 \times 0.038 = €6.884\ \text{million}$$

The currency swaps converts the \$10 million U.S. dollars to €6.884 million euros each year for seven years.

Creating Dual-Currency Bonds

A dual currency bond is a fixed-income instrument in which the coupon interest is paid in a different currency than the principal. An example would be a bond with a face value denominated in JPY, but the coupon payments are made in EUR. Given what we covered in the previous section about converting an annuity in one currency into an annuity in another currency using a currency swap, we can create a synthetic dual-currency bond where:

$$\text{Dual currency bond} = \text{Conventional bond} + \text{Currency swap (without exchanging NP)}$$

Creating a Synthetic Dual-Currency Bond

If an investor wants to invest in a dual-currency bond, but is unable to find a suitable instrument available in the market, he could create a synthetic security by combining a conventional bond with a currency swap.

Exhibit 2-4: Creating a Synthetic Dual-Currency Bond

Inception: $t = 0$

Each interest payment: $t = 1$ through T

Maturity: $t = T$

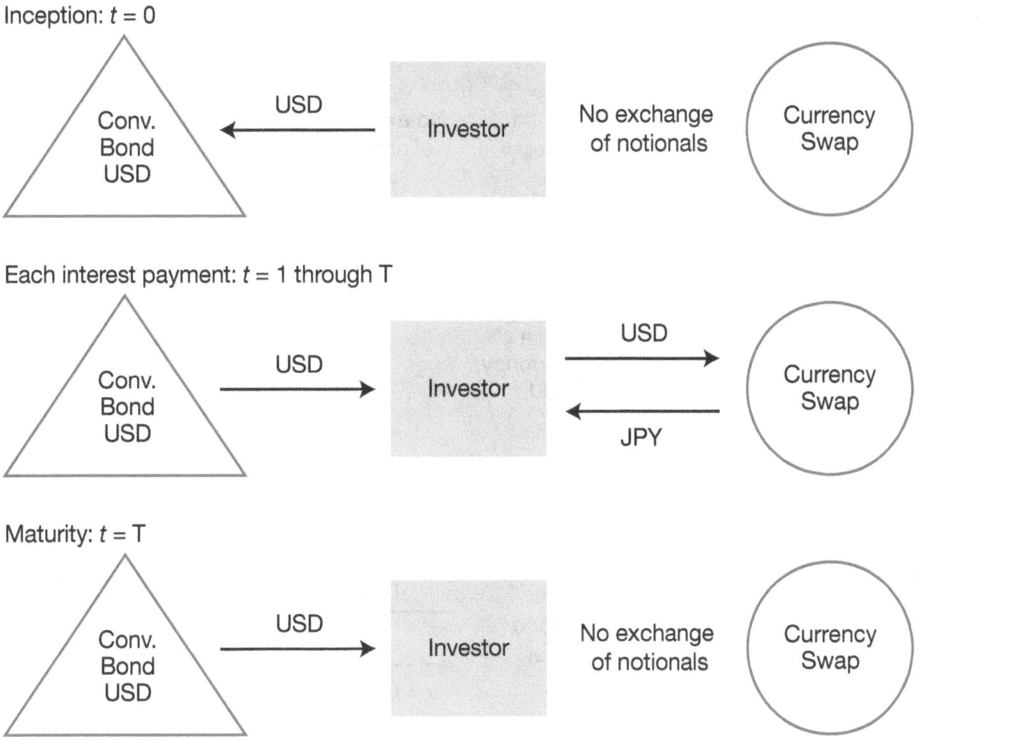

The investor has created a synthetic dual-currency bond by purchasing a conventional bond denominated in USD and simultaneously entering a swap to receive JPY and pay USD. However, at inception, notionals are not exchanged on the swap. On each coupon payment date, the conventional bond makes a payment in USD and the investor passes those payments through to the swap, receiving JPY in exchange. The swap has converted the USD bond payments into JPY payments. Finally, at maturity, the conventional bond returns principal but there are no notionals to be returned. By combining the conventional bond with a currency swap, the investor has effectively created a dual-currency bond with principal denominated in USD and payments denominated in JPY.

Issuing a Dual-Currency Bond

For a company that sells (issues) a dual-currency bond, the resulting short position can be offset by creating a long position in a synthetic dual-currency bond. For example, suppose a boutique investment banker wants to issue a dual-currency bond for a client where the principal is denominated in Hong Kong dollars (HKD) and the coupons are denominated in Chinese yuan renminbi (CNY).

At inception, the banker will issue the dual-currency note and simultaneously use the proceeds to purchase a conventional bond denominated in HKD. He will also enter a swap to exchange HKD for CNY but without exchanging notionals. At each payment date, the banker receives HKD from the conventional bond and exchanges it for CNY through the swap. The CNY payments on the swap can then be passed to the dualcurrency bondholder. Finally, at maturity, the conventional bond returns principal in HKD, which is then passed to the dual-currency bondholder. Since no notionals were exchanged at inception, there are none to be returned at swap expiration.

Exhibit 2-5: Issuing a Dual-Currency Bond

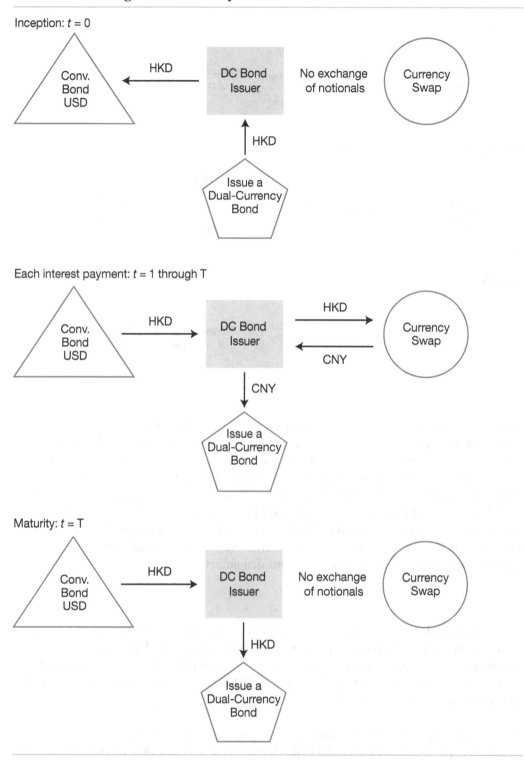

Effectively, the issuer has taken a short position by issuing a dual-currency bond and offset the risk by synthetically creating a long position in a similar instrument. The specific terms of each component (the interest rates on the dual-currency bond, the conventional bond, and each leg of the swap) will determine whether the issuer makes a net profit or loss on the deal.

Example 2-3

A Spanish firm has just issued a 12-year dual-currency bond with a principal amount of €60 million, paying coupons in USD. Based on the current exchange rate of USD 1.30 per EUR and a fixed bond coupon rate of 5 percent, the firm pays €60 × \$1.30/€ × 0.05 = \$3.9 million annual coupon. Which of the following interest rates will produce a positive net cash flow to the dual-currency bond issuer at each payment date?

	Conventional Bond	USD Leg of Swap	EUR Leg of Swap
A.	5.00 percent	5.00 percent	5.25 percent
B.	5.00 percent	5.25 percent	5.00 percent
C.	5.25 percent	5.00 percent	5.25 percent

Solution:

B.   A diagram of the swap payments will help illustrate the solution.

Each interest payment: $t = 1$ through T

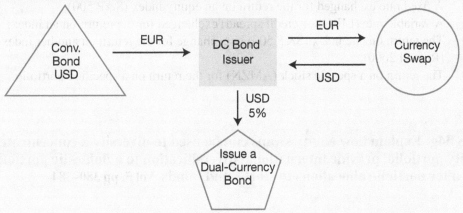

The issuer will have a net cash inflow if the interest rate on the USD leg of the swap exceeds 5 percent and the cash flows from the conventional bond and the EUR leg of the swap offset. Alternatively, if the interest rate on the USD leg of the swap matches the coupon payment on the dual-currency swap and the coupon from the conventional bond exceeds the rate on the EUR leg of the currency swap, the issuer will have a positive net cash flow. Choice A has a negative net cash flow. Choice C has a zero net cash flow. Choice B has a positive net cash flow because the rate applied to the USD leg of the swap exceeds the outflow applied to the dual-currency bond's coupon payment.

LESSON 3: STRATEGIES AND APPLICATIONS FOR MANAGING EQUITY MARKET RISK

Candidates should master the following hedging and speculation strategies:

Understand how to use *equity swaps* to:

- Synthetically diversify a concentrated portfolio.
- Synthetically achieve international diversification.
- Combine with bond swaps and synthetically change asset allocation between stocks and bonds.

EQUITY SWAPS

Like all swaps, an equity swap is a contract requiring the exchange of payments at preset dates. These swaps are unique in that at least one leg of the exchange is based on the return of an equity security or index. There are several configurations that are possible. For example:

- A fixed rate exchanged for the return on an equity index (S&P 500);
- A variable rate (LIBOR + credit spread) exchanged for the return on an index;
- The return on one index (S&P 500) in exchange for the return on another index (Russell 2000);
- The return on a specific stock (AMZN) for the return on a specified portfolio.

LOS 34g: Explain how equity swaps can be used to diversify a concentrated equity portfolio, provide international diversification to a domestic portfolio, and alter portfolio allocations to stocks and bonds. Vol 5, pp 380–384

Creating Diversification

Concentrated Holding

When a client is holding a large block of a single stock (or a large block of a few stocks), she might want to diversify the holdings by selling off some or all of the concentrated positions and use the funds from the sale to invest in a well-diversified portfolio. However, due to liquidity, legal, or other constraints, sale of a portion or all of the holdings might not be feasible or might only be feasible at a high cost.

An equity swap can be used in this situation to synthetically convert a concentrated portfolio to a diversified portfolio. Consider James Burns, the founder and CEO of Company X (CPX). The company went public several years ago and, while still thinly traded, has done well. Although he is very wealthy, Burns is concerned that virtually all of his wealth is held in CPX shares. He wants to diversify his holdings without actually selling shares, which he believes investors might interpret as his lack of confidence in the firm. His banker suggests an equity swap where he would pay the return on his CPX shares and receive the return on the Russell 2000.

Exhibit 3-1: Equity Swap to Diversify Concentrated Holding

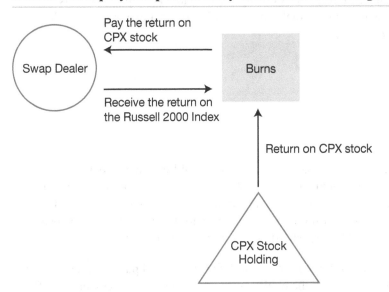

The swap effectively converts Burns' holding in CPX to a long position in the Russell 2000 index. A negative return on either of the underlying will simply reverse the direction of the cash flow. For example, a negative return on CPX stock during a period when the Russell 2000 has a positive return will result in the swap dealer paying Burns on both legs of the swap.

Example 3-1

Larry has just inherited $80 million worth of Oracle stock. While Larry is very happy with the newly found wealth, he realizes that it is essentially all of his wealth. He likes Oracle but intends to hold only $20 million of his shares. He would like to sell $60 million of the stock and invest the funds from the sale in the S&P 500 Index, but the will stipulates that he hold all shares for at least ten years.

1. Which of the following best describes the terms of the equity swap that Larry might use to diversify his Oracle holdings?

	Notional	Pay	Receive
A.	$80 million	Return on S&P 500 Index	Return on Oracle shares
B.	$60 million	Return on Oracle shares	Return on S&P 500 Index
C.	$60 million	Return on Oracle shares	Return on S&P 500 Index

2. If the return on the S&P 500 Index is 7 percent and the return on Oracle shares is 9 percent, Larry's net cash flow on the first annual payment of the swap is *closest* to:

   A. −1.6 million.
   B. −1.2 million.
   C. +1.2 million.

---

3. If the return on the S&P 500 Index during the second annual pay period is −2 percent and the return on Oracle shares is +3 percent, Larry's net cash flow on the swap is *closest* to:

   A. −3.0 million.
   B. −0.6 million.
   C. +0.6 million.

Solutions:

1. C. Larry wants to retain exposure to $20 million of his Oracle stock. Therefore, the appropriate notional should be $80 − $20 = $60 million. He is already receiving the return on Oracle shares in his portfolio so he wants to offset that by paying the return on Oracle in the swap. He wants to gain exposure to the Russell 2000, so he should receive the return on the index.

2. B. Larry will receive 7 percent on the S&P 500 Index and pay 9 percent on the shares in Oracle through the equity swap, making his net payment 7% − 9% = −2% on $60 million notional. His net payment will be 0.02($60 million) = $1.2 million cash *outflow*.

3. A. Larry receives the return on the S&P 500 Index and pays the return on Oracle stock. A negative return reverses the cash flow so that his net payment is −2% − 3% = −5%. The cash flow will be −0.05($60 million) = −$3.0 million.

The seemingly simple transaction works well in theory. However, in practice it may trigger some serious cash flow issues. First, holding a single stock like Oracle exposes him to a significant amount of unsystematic risk that does not present in a well-diversified portfolio such as the S&P 500 Index. Due to unsystematic risk, returns on the S&P 500 Index and returns on the Oracle stock can be of different signs. Cash flow issues arise when the returns on the S&P 500 Index are negative but the returns on the Oracle is positive. If it happens in the first quarter, the net cash flow to Larry is negative, which means that Larry needs to make a cash payment to the swap dealer. However, note that Larry has no other assets and he doesn't even have access to the $60 million of Oracle stock at the end of the third month. It makes it difficult for Larry to make the cash payment to keep the swap agreement ongoing.

The beta of Oracle stock is unlikely to be exactly one. Assuming it is greater than one, when the stock market experiences positive returns, returns on the Oracle stock are expected to be higher than that on the S&P 500 Index. Again, in such a situation, the net cash flow to Larry is negative, which brings constraints to Larry. It may force Larry to liquidate a portion of his Oracle holdings to satisfy the cash flow requirement. However, once he liquidates a portion of his Oracle holdings, he does not have a full $60 million spot holding to balance his $60 million leg of the Oracle position in the equity swap.

Larry's counterparty, the swap dealer, would certainly charge a fee for providing Larry the service. The fee may come from a reduced return on the S&P 500 Index, e.g., the swap dealer pays Larry the total return on the S&P 500 Index less 0.2 percent, or instead of paying Larry the total return, the swap dealer pays only the capital gains yield of the index to Larry.

Gaining International Exposure

An equity swap can also be used to convert a domestic portfolio to a global portfolio. The idea is very similar to diversifying a concentrated portfolio. For example, an insurance company's £100 million equity portfolio comprises only domestic, UK stocks. Its benchmark is the FTSE 100 Index. The investment committee has recently been educated about the merits of international diversification and instructs the portfolio manager to take immediate action to place 20 percent of the portfolio into international equities. The manager is concerned that the committee has not allowed for enough time to perform adequate research and decides to temporarily gain exposure through an equity swap. The terms of the swap are as follows:

- Notional: £20 million
- Payment frequency: Quarterly
- Pay: Return on the FTSE 100 Index
- Receive: Return on the MSCI World Index

The notional is 20 percent of the total portfolio value. Since the portfolio's benchmark should be a good proxy for its performance, the insurance company agrees to pay the return on the FTSE 100 Index, effectively passing the return on that portion of the portfolio through to the swap counterparty. In return, the insurance company receives the return on the MSCI World Index, gaining the exposure to international equities until it can properly research other investments.

Example 3-2

Amy Wise holds a $100 million portfolio that tracks the performance of the S&P 500 Index. Based on her research, Amy believes that in the next 12 months, Japan is expected to deliver superior returns. Amy intends to allocate $30 million of funds to participate in the market action in Japan. Transaction costs of liquidating $30 million of her U.S. equity and purchasing $30 million of Japanese equity are prohibitively high.

Design a swap strategy to assist Amy to achieve her diversification goal.

Solution:

We focus on the $30 million of Amy's U.S. equity holdings, the portion that Amy intends to convert to Japanese equity. An equity swap can be applied to assist Amy. The terms of the swap are listed below:

Negotiate an equity swap between the total holding period return on the S&P 500 Index and the total holding period return on the Nikkei 225 Index. Notional principal is $30 million. Tenor is 12 months. Settlement is quarterly.

In the equity swap, Amy pays the total return of the S&P 500 Index to the swap dealer and Amy receives the total return of the Nikkei 225 Index from the swap dealer. The total return is defined as the sum of dividend yield and capital gains yield over the quarterly holding period.

$$\text{Cash flow to Amy} = \$30\,\text{million} \times (\text{Return on Nikkei}\,225 - \text{Return on S\&P}\,500)$$

> Because Amy receives returns on the S&P 500 Index from her stock holdings, the equity swap transforms her returns on her stock portfolio to returns on the Nikkei 225 Index. The equity swap helps Amy to achieve diversification on $30 million stock holdings.

Alter a Portfolio's Asset Allocation

The basic premise of using swaps to alter the behavior of a portfolio is to offset the exposure you don't want with one leg of the swap and assume the swap leg with the exposure you do want. For example, a $250 million portfolio is currency allocated 50 percent to stocks and 50 percent to bonds. The portfolio's corresponding benchmarks are the MSCI World Index and the Merrill Lynch Global Bond Index, respectively. The portfolio manager wants to make a tactical allocation to 20 percent stocks, 60 percent bonds, and 20 percent real estate, instead of incurring substantial transaction costs, using a series of one-year swaps.

	Stocks	Bonds	NCREIF Property Index
Current allocation	$125 million	$125 million	$ 0 million
Desired allocation	$ 50 million	$150 million	$50 million
Change in allocation	−$ 75 million	$ 25 million	$50 million

The portfolio manager must reduce her exposure to stocks by $75 million by entering a swap to *pay* the return on the MSCI World Index (the portfolio's benchmark) on the same amount of notional and receive LIBOR. Similarly, she must increase her exposure to bonds by entering a swap to *receive* the return on the Merrill Lynch Global Bond Index with a $25 million notional and pay LIBOR. Finally, she must enter a third swap to *receive* the return on the NCREIF Property Index and pay LIBOR on $50 million notional.

The LIBOR exposures cancel each other out [LIBOR(+75 million − 25 million − 50 million) = 0], leaving the portfolio with the appropriate exposures to match the desired asset allocation.

Example 3-3

A portfolio manager holds a $500 million portfolio. The current allocation is 70 percent in stocks and remaining 30 percent in bonds. Of the 70 percent stock holdings, 40 percent is in small cap stocks and 60 percent is in large cap stocks. Of the 30 percent bond holdings, 20 percent is in Treasuries and 80 percent is in corporate bonds.

Recent fundamental analysis prompts the portfolio manager to perform a tactical change in asset allocation. The target allocation involves 80 percent of assets in stocks and 20 percent in bonds. Of the 80 percent in stocks, 60 percent is in small cap stocks and 40 percent is in large cap stocks. Of the 20 percent in bonds, 50 percent is in Treasuries and 50 percent is in corporates.

Explain how the manager might achieve the tactical allocation using swaps.

Solution:

The following table lists the current and target asset allocation across stocks and bonds.

	Current ($million)	Target ($million)	Net Change ($million)
Small cap	140	240	Buy 100
Large cap	210	160	Sell 50
Treasuries	30	50	Buy 20
Corporates	120	50	Sell 70

Due to high transaction costs and other factors, the portfolio manager is most likely using equity and bond swaps to synthetically change the asset allocation. The following positions may help the portfolio manager to achieve his goal:

- A swap where the portfolio manager receives returns on small-cap stock index and pays returns on large-cap stock index. NP = $50 million.
- A swap where the portfolio manager receives returns on small-cap stock index and pays returns on a corporate bond index. NP = $50 million.
- A swap where the portfolio manager receives returns on a Treasury bond index and pays returns on a corporate bond index. NP = $20 million.

LESSON 4: STRATEGIES AND APPLICATIONS USING SWAPTIONS

Candidates should master the following hedging and speculation strategies:

Understand how to use *interest rate swaptions* to:

- Hedge against adverse interest rate movements in anticipation of a future borrowing.
- Synthetically terminate an existing interest rate swap.
- Synthetically add or remove embedded call/put options in a bond.

LOS 34h: Demonstrate the use of an interest rate swaption 1) to change the payment pattern of an anticipated future loan and 2) to terminate a swap. Vol 5, pp 389–397

Swaptions

A swaption is an option that gives the holder the right, but not the obligation, to enter a swap at a future date. The terms of the underlying swap are determined at the inception of the option contract. Like swaps themselves, swaptions are customized instruments whose terms may be negotiated to suit each counterparty's needs. The notation used to refer to a swaption is *FS*(start period, end period), where the start period corresponds to the expiration of the swaption and the end period corresponds to the expiration of the underlying swap. For example, if the underlying swap has a tenor of three years and the swaption expires in one year, the notation referencing this swaption would be *FS*(1,4).

There are two types of swaptions, a *payer* swaption and a *receiver* swaption. An American-style payer swaption holder has the right to enter an interest rate swap at any time during the life of the swaption as the fixed-rate payer paying the exercise rate specified in the swaption contract. It is advantageous to the payer swaption holder to exercise the swaption when the fixed swap rate is *higher* than the exercise rate.

Similarly, an American-style receiver swaption holder has the right to enter an interest rate swap at any time during the life of the swaption as the fixed-rate receiver receiving the exercise rate specified in the swaption contract. It is advantageous to the receiver swaption holder to exercise the swaption when the fixed swap rate is *lower* than the exercise rate.

From the definition of payer swaptions, we understand that when interest rates are high, swap rates are high, payer swaptions are in-the-money. When interest rates are high, fixed-rate bond prices are low. So indirectly, payer swaptions can be viewed as *put options on fixed-rate bonds*.

From the definition of receiver swaptions, we understand that when interest rates are low, swap rates are low, receiver swaptions are in-the-money. When interest rates are low, fixed-rate bond prices are high. So indirectly, receiver swaptions can be viewed as *call options on fixed-rate bonds*.

> Receiver swaption = Call option on a bond
> Payer swaption = Put option on a bond

As in the preceding sections, we take a closer look at particular applications of swaptions.

Hedging Future Borrowing

Suppose a firm knows today that it will need to borrow at a later date to finance a future project. It might anticipate that its banker will insist on a floating-rate loan, although the firm prefers the certainty of borrowing at a fixed rate. Furthermore, the project has a positive NPV at current interest rates but, if interest rates were to rise before the financing is finalized, it might not remain an attractive investment. How might the firm address these concerns?

Answer: purchase a payer swaption. The payer swaption allows the holder to enter as the fixed-rate payer (long position) on a plain vanilla interest rate swap. When the firm takes out the floating-rate loan with its bank, it exercises the swaption, offsetting the variable rate and paying a fixed rate. Thus, the firm converts floating debt to fixed debt and locks in the fixed rate at the time the option is negotiated. However, it will have to pay a premium for this protection.

The basic idea of hedging future borrowing is straightforward. However, execution of the loan + swaption strategy requires attention to many details. We use an example to demonstrate this use of swaptions.

Company X (CPX) intends to borrow $6 million two years from now. The firm prefers to borrow at fixed rates, but knows its banker insists on floating. CPX has used swaps to convert its floating-rate debt to fixed and finds the current swap rates attractive at 5.00 percent. However, the firm's CFO is concerned that swap rates might rise dramatically over the next year. The loan terms are LIBOR percent, payable semiannually for three years.

A swap dealer offers an American payer swaption on an underlying swap, *FS*(2,5), with an exercise rate of 5.25 percent. The underlying swap's variable rate is LIBOR. The premium required to purchase the swaption is $76,500.

Over the next two years, interest rates moved as shown in the following table.

3-Year Plain Vanilla Interest Rate Swaps

Period	Swap Rates
0	5.25%
6-mos.	5.00%
12-mos.	5.20%
18-mos.	5.25%
24-mos.	5.50%

If CPX accepts the dealer's offer, it will incur an immediate cash outflow of $76,500 as the premium on the swaption. At the end of two years, swap rates have risen above the swaption exercise rate of 5.25 percent, putting the payer swaption in-the-money at a prevailing swap rate of 5.50 percent. CPX will exercise the swaption, take out the loan at LIBOR, and enter a three-year swap to pay 5.25 percent fixed and receive LIBOR. Thus, CPX will have converted a floating-rate loan to a fixed-rate loan and done so at the favorable rate that prevailed at the time the swaption was negotiated.

Other details to note include:

- The swaption may be cash settled at expiration instead of actually entering the swap;
- If swap rates had instead fallen over the two years preceding the execution of the loan, CPX would simply allow the swaption to expire without exercising it and instead enter a swap at the prevailing rate, but the premium would still be forfeit;
- If CPX had decided to accelerate its plans and take out the loan after only one year, the American swaption may be exercised at any time before expiration, while a European swaption may only be exercised at expiration.

Example 4-1

Firm Z (FMZ) is scheduled to roll over €8 million of three-year debt at a variable rate of EURIBOR maturing one year from now. Although it finds borrowing at variable rates to be convenient, FMZ converts all its floating-rate debt to fixed-rate debt using plain vanilla interest rate swaps. While the current swap rate of 4.50 percent is attractive, FMZ's CFO is concerned that it might rise dramatically by the end of the year. She is considering using a swaption with an exercise rate of 4.75 percent to hedge the risk of rising swap rates.

1. To hedge the risk of rising swap rates, FMZ should:

    A. buy a receiver swaption.
    B. buy a payer swaption.
    C. sell a payer swaption.

---

2. Under which of the following prevailing swap rates would FMZ choose to exercise its swaption?

    A. Swap rate < 4.50 percent.
    B. Swap rate > 4.75 percent.
    C. Swap rate = 4.75 percent.

3. FMZ would *most likely* prefer an American-style swaption over a European-style swaption if it intends to:

    A. roll the old debt over at maturity.
    B. retire the old debt at maturity.
    C. refinance the debt before maturity.

Solutions:

1. B. The firm should buy a payer swaption to hedge the risk of interest rate increases, which gives FMZ the right but not the obligation to enter a swap as the fixed-rate payer.

2. B. The swaption will be in-the-money at prevailing swap rates above the exercise rate of 4.75 percent. FMZ will only exercise the option if it is in-the-money.

3. C. An American-style swaption may be exercised at any time before expiration, while a European swaption may only be exercised at expiration. If the firm thinks it might want to refinance the loan prior to maturity, the more flexible American option is the most appropriate style.

Terminate an Existing Swap

Another application of swaptions is to terminate an existing interest rate swap. Banks often prefer to lend at floating rates as a way to mitigate interest rate risk. Borrowers, on the other hand, often prefer the certainty of fixed-rate debt. As we've seen, an interest rate swap can be used by the borrower to convert floating-rate debt into fixed-rate debt. However, if interest rates suddenly trend down, the borrower might regret its decision and wish to exit the swap.

There are only a couple of ways to exit a swap *before* expiration. One way is to negotiate early termination with the counterparty, which will likely involve a cash payment of the swap's value. The alternative is to enter another swap that offsets the original swap. By purchasing a swaption on this offset swap at the time the original swap is entered, the borrower preserves the option of exiting the swap should circumstances make floating-rate debt preferable.

Consider our friends at Company X (CPX) who borrow for three years at LIBOR and enter a fixed-for-floating interest rate swap to convert their variable-rate loan into fixed-rate debt. However, if interest rates trend down, CPX wants to exit the swap. So, at the time it takes out the loan and enters the swap, the firm also purchases an American-style receiver swaption, which gives it the right but not the obligation to enter a new swap as the fixed-rate receiver (floating-rate payer).

Exhibit 4-1: Initiation of Loan + Swap + Receiver Swaption

2. CPX simultaneously enters a swap to pay fixed and receive floating, converting its floating-rate loan into fixed-rate debt.

3. At the same time, CPX purchases an American-style receiver swaption to offset the original swap.

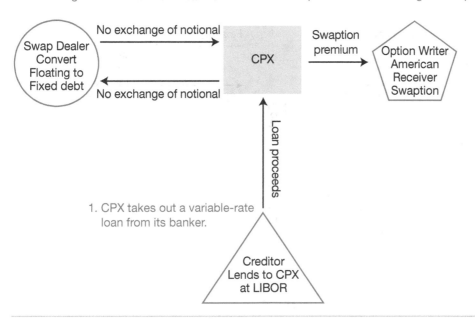

1. CPX takes out a variable-rate loan from its banker.

Looking at Exhibit 4-1, the net cash flow when the loan is taken out is the loan proceeds less the swaption premium. Recall there is no exchange of notionals at the initiation of an interest rate swap.

As long as the prevailing swap rate remains above the exercise rate on the swaption, CPX will not exercise and the cash flows will work as we saw with a conversion of floating-to-fixed-rate debt. However, if the prevailing swap rate falls below the exercise rate on the swaption and CPX expects them to remain low (or even drift lower), it will exercise the swaption as shown in Exhibit 4-2.

Exhibit 4-2: Exercise of Swaption

2. The original swap remains in place under the same terms without change.

3. Exercising the receiver swaption adds a new swap that offsets the original swap, leaving a floating-rate payment to the creditor.

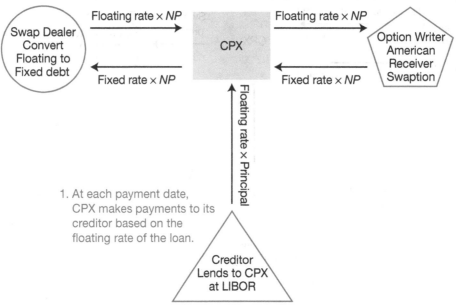

1. At each payment date, CPX makes payments to its creditor based on the floating rate of the loan.

Example 4-2

Firm W is currently engaged in an interest rate swap where the firm pays a floating rate, LIBOR, and receives a fixed rate of 4 percent. The swap expires five years from now. Payments are settled semiannually and the notional principal of the swap is $8 million. The firm wants the flexibility to terminate the swap at any time during the life of the contract.

1. Which of the following swaptions would *most likely* meet Firm W's requirements in facilitating early termination of its existing swap agreement?

    A. Buy a European-style payer swaption.
    B. Sell an American-style receiver swaption.
    C. Buy an American-style payer swaption.

2. Assume the exercise rate of the swaption is 5 percent and that at any time t, before the end of Year 5, $F(t,5)$ is the swap fixed rate for an interest rate swap that starts at time t and ends at Year 5. Firm W would *most likely* exercise its swaption if:

    A. $F(t,5) < 5$ percent.
    B. $F(t,5) > 5$ percent.
    C. $F(t,5) = 5$ percent.

3. The swaption payoff if the exercise rate is 5 percent and the prevailing swap rate, $F(t,5)$, is 6 percent is *closest* to:

   A. −1.0%
   B. 0.0%
   C. +1.0%

Solutions:

1. C. The firm should buy a payer swaption to have the option to terminate the existing interest rate swap where the firm is the fixed rate receiver. In the future, when interest rates are low, the existing (pay floating receive fixed) swap generates gains. However, the payer swaption is out-of-the-money and does not hurt the firm. When interest rates are high, the existing (pay floating receive fixed) swap generates losses. The payer swaption is in-the-money and hedges away the loss.

2. B. The payer swaption is American style and can be exercised at any time before its expiration at the end of Year 5. At any time t on or before the end of Year 5, if the prevailing swap fixed rate $F(t,5)$ is higher than the payer swaption's exercise rate of 5 percent, the swaption is in-the-money and will likely be exercised at that point in time t.

   To terminate the existing swap at time t, the firm should enter a new interest rate swap where the firm receives LIBOR and pays fixed rate $F(t,5)$. Note that this swap has a zero value at its initiation time t.

3. A. Consider the cash flows:

Swap	Swaption
Pay floating	Receive floating
Receive fixed at 4%	Pay fixed at 5%

   The floating payments cancel and the fixed payments, receive 4% and pay 5%, result in a net outflow of 1%.

Add or Remove Embedded Options in a Bond

Bond prices move inversely with interest rates. So, as interest rates fall, bond prices rise. Recall also that a call option gives the owner the right, but not the obligation, to purchase the underlying at the strike price. As the underlying's price rises, the value of the call option increases. For example, a call option on a bond would increase in value as the price of the underlying bond rose and interest rates fell. We also saw that the value of a receiver swaption also rises as interest rates fall. We can therefore conclude that:

> Receiver swaption – Call option on bond

Similarly, a put option increases in value as the price of the underlying falls. For example, a put option on a bond would increase in value when the underlying bond's price falls, which occurs when interest rates rise. Since a payer swaption increases in value as interest rates rise, we can conclude that:

> Payer swaption = Put option on bond

Recall that a callable bond may be repurchased by the issuer at the call price, which it will do if interest rates fall and the existing debt can be replaced with cheaper debt. The embedded call option benefits the issuer, who effectively owns the option to call the issue back. The bondholder effectively sells the call option to the issuer and reaps a higher yield as a premium.

> Callable bond = Straight bond − Call option on bond

A putable bond gives the bondholder the right to return the bond to the issuer and reclaim his principal, which he will do if interest rates rise and he can reinvest at more attractive rates. Since the embedded put option benefits the bondholder, the bondholder effectively buys the put from the issuer paying a premium in the form of a lower yield.

> Putable bond = Straight bond + Put option on bond

Replacing the call/put options with receiver/payer swaptions, we derive the recipe for manipulating embedded call and put options on bonds using swaptions:

> Callable bond = Straight bond − Receiver swaption
> Putable bond = Straight bond + Payer swaption

The key to understanding this section is the two equations above and their simple algebraic transformations. We list all four equations below:

> Callable bond = Straight bond − Receiver swaption
> −Callable bond = Receiver swaption − Straight bond
> Putable bond = Straight bond + Payer swaption
> −Putable bond = −Straight bond − Payer swaption

The first two equations are more important than the last two equations because there are clearly more callable bonds in the bond market than putable bonds. So here we only cover callable bonds. You should interpret positive signs as long positions and negative signs as short positions.

Monetizing an Embedded Call

Suppose CPX has an outstanding callable bond paying a fixed rate, r_0, but does not expect the call to be exercised before the issue matures. It is effectively paying for an embedded call option that it never expects to use. CPX can use a receiver swaption to synthetically sell (remove) the bond issue's embedded call option by receiving an immediate premium. The issuer is short the callable bond and wants to convert it to a straight bond. Drawing from our list of key equations:

> (2a) −Callable bond = −Straight bond + Receiver swaption
>
> (2b) −Straight bond = −Callable bond − Receiver swaption

We can see in Equation 2b that a short position in a callable bond can be synthetically converted to a short position in a straight bond by selling a receiver swaption with an appropriate strike rate equal to the current bond issue's fixed rate less an appropriate credit spread ($X = r_0 - s$).

If interest rates remain stable, the bond issue is never called and the swaption is never exercised. The issue matures, the swaption expires, and the issuer keeps the swaption premium, monetizing its embedded call option and reducing its cost of debt to that of a noncallable bond.

If, on the other hand, interest rates do fall, the bond will be called and the swaption will be exercised. While the issuer, CPX, can refinance the debt at a lower prevailing rate, it must still make periodic payments on the new swap resulting from the receiver swaption holder's exercise. Furthermore, CPX must enter a second swap as the floating rate payer to offset the floating rate it is receiving on the first swap (from the swaption's exercise). This second swap's fixed rate is the prevailing swap rate at the time of exercise, $F(t,T)$.

Exhibit 4-3 illustrates the cash flows if the prevailing interest rate falls below the strike rate [$F(t,T) < X$], triggering both CPX's call of the bond issue and the exercise of the swaption.

Exhibit 4-3: Prevailing Swap Rate Falls Below Strike, $F(t,T) < X$

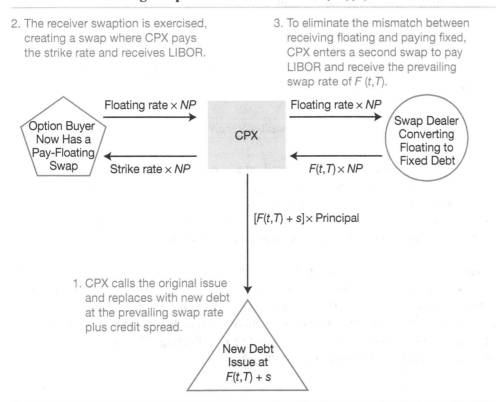

2. The receiver swaption is exercised, creating a swap where CPX pays the strike rate and receives LIBOR.

3. To eliminate the mismatch between receiving floating and paying fixed, CPX enters a second swap to pay LIBOR and receive the prevailing swap rate of $F(t,T)$.

Floating rate × NP

Floating rate × NP

Option Buyer Now Has a Pay-Floating Swap

CPX

Swap Dealer Converting Floating to Fixed Debt

Strike rate × NP

$F(t,T) × NP$

$[F(t,T) + s] ×$ Principal

1. CPX calls the original issue and replaces with new debt at the prevailing swap rate plus credit spread.

New Debt Issue at $F(t,T) + s$

The net cash flow of all these payments is:

$$
\begin{aligned}
NCF &= NP \times [-\text{New bond fixed rate} + \text{LIBOR} - \text{Strike rate} + \text{Prevailing swap rate} - \text{LIBOR}] \\
&= NP \times \{-[F(t,T)+s] + \text{LIBOR} - X + F(t,T) - \text{LIBOR}\} \\
&= NP \times [-X - s] = NP \times [-(r_0 - s) - s] = NP(r_0)
\end{aligned}
$$

The effective interest rate that CPX pays on its debt is the strike rate plus the credit spread. However, recall that the strike rate is given by the fixed rate on the original bond less the credit spread. Since the issuer monetized the call, if interest rates unexpectedly fall, CPX does not enjoy lower payments associated with refinancing the debt. However, it did collect the swaption premium, which lowered its overall cost of debt to that of a noncallable bond.

Some details to highlight:

- The exercise (strike) rate on the receiver swaption should exclude the bond's credit spread. For example, if the original bond was issued with a fixed rate of 6 percent, which includes a 1.75 percent credit spread, the appropriate exercise rate on the receiver swaption should be 6 − 1.75 = 4.25 percent.
- The swaption premium effectively reduces the issuer's cost of debt, making it comparable to a noncallable bond.
- If the swaption is in-the-money, it will be exercised and the issuer will call the debt, refinance it at the prevailing swap rate plus a credit spread, and enter a second swap to receive fixed at the prevailing swap rate.
- Except for the swaption premium, the issuer will not benefit from the lower rates associated with refinancing the debt.

Creating a Synthetic Embedded Call

Referring back to Equation 2a, a bond issuer can also synthetically add a call option to a bond by purchasing a receiver swaption.

$$
\text{(2a)} \quad -\text{Callable bond} = -\text{Straight bond} + \text{Receiver swaption}
$$

Again, a receiver swaption is effectively a call on a bond. If interest rates never fall below the strike rate, the option is never in-the-money, expires worthless, and the bond issuer forfeits the premium. The added cost of the premium represents the cost associated with having issued a callable bond in the first place. As before, the appropriate strike rate is the current fixed rate on the bond (r_0) less the relevant credit spread.

If the prevailing interest rate [$F(t,T)$] falls below the strike rate ($X = r_0 - s$), the receiver swaption is exercised, and the issuer enters a swap to receive a fixed payment in exchange for making a floating-rate payment (LIBOR). The swap created by the swaption leaves CPX with an unwanted floating rate outflow, which it eliminates by entering a second swap to pay the prevailing fixed rate [$F(t,T)$] and receive floating. The cash flows when the swaption is exercised are illustrated in Exhibit 4-4.

Exhibit 4-4: Synthetically Calling a Noncallable Bond, $F(t,T) < X$

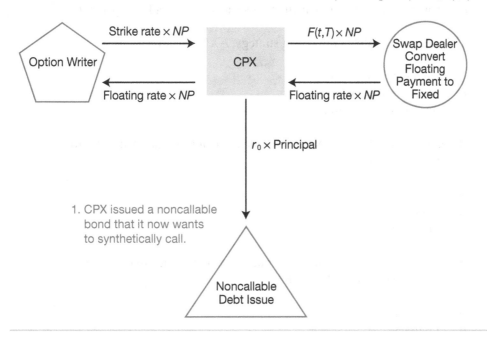

2. CPX exercises its receiver swaption, entering a swap with the option writer as the fixed-rate receiver.

3. To offset the floating rate outflow, CPX enters a second swap to pay fixed at the prevailing swap rate, $F(t,T)$.

1. CPX issued a noncallable bond that it now wants to synthetically call.

The net cash flow of all these payments is:

$$NCF = NP \times [-\text{Noncallable bond fixed rate} - (\text{LIBOR} + \text{Strike rate} - \text{Prevailing swap rate} + \text{LIBOR})$$
$$= NP \times [-r_0 - \text{LIBOR} + X - F(t,T) + \text{LIBOR}] = -r_0 + (r_0 - s) - F(t,T)$$
$$= NP \times -[F(t,T) + s]$$

So, after exercising the swaption and entering two swaps, the net interest rate paid by CPX is the prevailing swap rate plus a credit spread, which is lower than the original interest rate paid on the noncallable debt. As long as the deal is structured to match the coupon dates and maturities, CPX has effectively called the debt and replaced it with cheaper financing.

Example 4-3

Axme Corp (AXC) has a $75 million noncallable debt issue outstanding and would like the option of calling the bonds in two years if interest rates warrant refinancing. The debt carries a coupon rate of 9 percent, which includes a credit spread of 2 percent.

1. To implement its debt conversion strategy, AXC should:

    A. sell a receiver swaption.
    B. buy a receiver swaption.
    C. buy a payer swaption.

2. Based solely on the information provided, the appropriate strike rate for the swaption is *closest* to:

    A. 2 percent.
    B. 7 percent.
    C. 9 percent.

3. If in two years the prevailing swap rate is 5 percent, the effective periodic coupon rate paid on the debt will be *closest* to:

    A. 5 percent.
    B. 7 percent.
    C. 9 percent.

Solutions:

1. B. The conversion of noncallable debt into callable debt is based on the following relationship:

    $$-\text{Callable bond} = -\text{Straight bond} + \text{Receiver swaption}$$

    Therefore, to convert a straight bond into a callable bond, the issuer must purchase a receiver swaption.

2. B. The strike rate for the receiver swaption should reflect interest rate risk, but not credit risk. Therefore, the appropriate strike rate would be the current bond coupon rate less the relevant credit spread. Since we are given no information to imply that AXC's credit quality has changed, it is appropriate to apply a 2 percent spread, giving a strike rate of $X = r_0 - s = 9\% - 2\% = 7\%$..

3. B. The swaption will be exercised if the prevailing swap rate $F(t,7)$ falls below the strike rate ($X = r_0 - s$), which is indeed the case here. Drawing the swap diagram might be the most effective approach to solving swap questions. The net cash flow analysis indicates that the effective periodic coupon rate after exercising: $NCF = NP \times -[F(t,T) + s] = NP \times -(5 + 2) = NP \times -(7\%)$. By exercising its synthetic call, AXC has effectively refinanced to debt that is 200 basis points cheaper than its actual issue.